Medical Tourism

Recent Titles in Health and Medical Issues Today

Organ Donation, Sarah Boslaugh
Food Inequalities, Tennille Nicole Allen
Internet Addiction, Kathryn Vercillo

Medical Tourism

Lydia Gan

BLOOMSBURY ACADEMIC
NEW YORK • LONDON • OXFORD • NEW DELHI • SYDNEY

BLOOMSBURY ACADEMIC
Bloomsbury Publishing Inc, 1385 Broadway, New York, NY 10018, USA
Bloomsbury Publishing Plc, 50 Bedford Square, London, WC1B 3DP, UK
Bloomsbury Publishing Ireland, 29 Earlsfort Terrace, Dublin 2, D02 AY28, Ireland

First published in the United States of America 2025

A catalog record for this book is available from the Library of Congress.

ISBN: HB: 979-8-2161-7034-1
ePDF: 979-8-2161-7035-8
eBook: 979-8-2161-7036-5

Series: Health and Medical Issues Today

Typeset by Newgen KnowledgeWorks Pvt. Ltd., Chennai, India
Printed and bound in the United States of America

For product safety related questions contact productsafety@bloomsbury.com.

To find out more about our authors and books visit www.bloomsbury.com and sign up for our newsletters.

For Robert and Rea

Contents

Series Foreword

Every day, the public is bombarded with information on developments in medicine and health care. Whether it is on the latest techniques in treatment or research or on concerns over public health threats, this information directly affects the lives of people more than almost any other issue. Although there are many sources for understanding these topics—from websites and blogs to newspapers and magazines—students and ordinary citizens often need one resource that makes sense of the complex health and medical issues affecting their daily lives.

The Health and Medical Issues Today series provides just such a one-stop resource for obtaining a solid overview of the most controversial areas of health care in the twenty-first century. Each volume addresses one topic and provides a balanced summary of what is known. These volumes provide an excellent first step for students and laypeople interested in understanding how health care works in our society today.

Each volume is broken into several parts to provide readers and researchers with easy access to the information they need:

Part I provides overview chapters on background information—including chapters on such areas as the historical, scientific, medical, social, and legal issues involved—that a citizen needs to intelligently understand the topic.

Part II provides capsule examinations of the most heated contemporary issues and debates and analyzes in a balanced manner the viewpoints held by various advocates in the debates.

Part III provides case studies that show examples of the concepts discussed in the previous parts.

A directory of resources and a glossary provide additional reference material and serve as the best next step in learning about the topic at hand.

The Health and Medical Issues Today series strives to provide readers with all the information needed to begin making sense of some of the most important debates going on in the world today. The series includes volumes on topics such as stem cell research, obesity, gene therapy, alternative medicine, organ transplantation, and more.

Preface

What is medical tourism? It is simply an act of traveling outside your country of residence for medical services. It is an industry defined by multifaceted players—the patients or the medical tourists, the destination healthcare facilities, the payers or insurance companies, the agents or middlemen, and everyone in between who is involved in the business one way or another. Chapter 1 reviews these players and their market roles. There are many reasons why one would embark on such a healing journey outside one's home country, as discussed in Chapter 2. Mine has always been a natural and convenient one. After spending nine years teaching at an elite university in Singapore, my family consciously moved back to the United States in 2007. Since then, I have spent every summer traveling and visiting friends and families in Singapore and Malaysia. I must confess that I'm inclined to experiment with various therapies while on vacation, feeling more relaxed. Blessed with a strong US currency, I began undertaking an annual physical examination (popular in that region as a preventive measure) and taking advantage of various affordable treatments such as dental, cosmetic, and even acupuncture while traveling to that part of the world. That was my first taste of medical tourism. As I advanced my research into the fascinating topic of medical tourism, I expanded my summer travel plan each year by stopping over at "halfway" cities, such as Istanbul, Amman, and Johannesburg, to name just a few. The intention was to tour and interview some of those world-class hospitals and, at the same time, take in some local sightseeing. I visited the hospitals for research purposes on numerous occasions, and occasionally, I checked myself in as an outpatient to "test" the local healthcare systems. I find the traveling part fascinating, from watching the bizarre scene of a helicopter landing on the parking lot along with other parked cars in South Africa to getting an ophthalmologic appointment within twelve hours after my plane has landed in Singapore to being placed in front of the line while checked in as an international patient at a healthcare facility in Jerusalem. The experiences, along with their potential adventures, seem endlessly inviting. Before I realized this, I had visited a dozen hospitals in half a dozen countries, and the experience has undoubtedly enriched my research work. My medical tourism experience was from a researcher's or convenient patient's perspective. To me, travel seems to come first before the medical part. This is undoubtedly quite different from the conventional definition of medical tourism, that is, planning a trip mainly for medical purposes.

Like many across the country, I have lost numerous loved ones to cancer. In the United States, cancer has become the second leading cause of death next to heart disease, and health experts have predicted it will soon catch up with heart disease. Inundated by this fact, I began to research complementary and alternative medicine, particularly in natural cancer treatments. These alternative therapies are discussed in Chapter 3. Complementary and alternative medicine opens a new avenue of exciting research with more promising outcomes than conventional medicine in some cases. It turns out that brand-name US medical centers have already embraced the idea of integrative medicine in the last three decades. It combines conventional and nonconventional approaches to treatment, working together to offer patients the best alternatives, complementing each other's needs or offsetting each other's deficiencies. It provides holistic care for the body, spirit, and mind. The use of acupuncture, essential oils, nutrition, and supplements, among others, have proved to be ideal complementary therapies for cancer patients. While an estimated 50 percent of US teenagers have faced severe mental illnesses, anxiety, and depression at some point in their lives, an increasing number of them were open to wellness approaches such as yoga and meditation to unwind. In the area of interstate medical tourism, the use of medical cannabis holds endless potential for research as well as medical remedies for many who suffer from serious ailments or chronic pains. These are reviewed in the second half of Chapter 6, and their related regulatory and ethical issues are considered in Chapter 9.

It is essential to learn about medical tourism because it is a promising industry with the potential to extend into integrative medicine that is anticipated to serve all ages in the United States and globally. Moreover, it provides a viable medical option for those underinsured or uninsured, those unable to access specific medical procedures or products, and those who value faster access or confidentiality or more personalized care or vacationing opportunities. All are important in terms of consumer and patient sovereignty. Further, it allows Americans to access quality care and relieves the strain on public resources for the sick at home. For those who have never used medical tourism, Chapters 4 and 5 are helpful chapters to get acquainted with who the healthcare providers are and what value-added services the middlemen may provide. Once convinced about making a medical trip, Chapters 7, 8, and the first half of Chapter 9 are excellent reads on patients' concerns, how the insurance companies may be involved, and deeper issues to consider when things go wrong. Chapter 10 discusses the more significant and long-term impacts of medical tourism on host countries, home countries, and its future trends. Medical tourism raises the gross domestic product of destination countries mainly by improving trickle-down economic development and preventing the external brain drain of healthcare professionals. Most of its impacts on home countries have directly affected the home healthcare systems, politically, socially, and economically, and they do not necessarily affect an individual patient in the immediate short term. Nevertheless, as an informed citizen, one should be aware and care about how this nascent industry may impact one's home country.

Acknowledgments

I have had the privilege of visiting umpteen world-class hospitals and interviewing their administrators since I started my research work on medical tourism nearly two decades ago. First, I would like to thank Joan Henderson, my then colleague at Nanyang Technological University, Singapore, for her pioneer work on the subject and for introducing me to it; Jim Frederick, for his collaborative work; and David Boucher of Bumrungrad Hospital, Thailand, for his enthusiasm on the subject and his referrals to many of these hospitals.

Second, I want to thank the following individuals for their valuable time either in coordinating or giving a hospital tour or interviewing with me, both in person and virtually: Dina Kattan of Jordan; Shereen Manneh of Specialty Hospital, Amman, Jordan; Hashem Irshaid and Amani Khartan of Jordan Hospital, Amman, Jordan; Azzam Ibrahim of Al Khalidi Medical Center, Amman, Jordan; Raya Mizrachi of Hadassah Medical Center, Jerusalem, Israel; Leyla Ataoglu and Ilyas Benveniste of Acibadem Healthcare Group, Istanbul, Turkey; Dilek Inci and Burcu Dagistanli of Anadolu Medical Centre, Istanbul, Turkey; Lih-Yi Soo of Raffles Hospital, Singapore; Sue Lee and Edgar Toral of Sime Darby Medical Center, Ara Damansara, Malaysia; Nadiah Wan of Sunway Medical Centre Berhad, Subang Jaya, Malaysia; Kinam Jin of South Korea Council of Medical Tourism, Seoul, South Korea; Julia Hong of Nanoori International Spine and Joints Hospital, Seoul, South Korea; Liezl Furlong of Mediclinic Sandton, Bryanston, South Africa; Lorraine Melvill of Surgeon and Safari, Bryanston, South Africa.

Third, I want to thank the CAM 2023: Many Paths to Wellness Conference and Ann Fonfa, its organizer and founder of the Annie Appleseed Project. Their introduction to the topic of complementary and alternative medicine, as well as various modes of alternative cancer treatments, has been invaluable. I am particularly thankful to Henning Saupe, MD, and Zubin Marolia, MD, for their inspiring guidance on natural cancer treatment protocols and to George Wong for his insights on the practice and efficacy of traditional Chinese medicine.

Lastly, I sincerely thank my dedicated research assistants, Ethan Gartner, Juanita Borges, and Cyra Lowery. I also thank Terry MacAlmon for his inspiring piano instrumental musics, *Night Sounds: Liquid Love* and *Night Sounds II: In the Quiet*, which provided a soothing background as I spent countless hours writing this book.

Part I

Overview

1

The Basics of Medical Tourism

What do surgeon, sea, and sand have in common in white sandy Phuket Island of Thailand? What do a surgeon and safari have in common in South Africa? This chapter defines medical tourism, what it is internationally and domestically, and what it is not. The value and growth of medical tourism will then be estimated from various sources. The detailed historical development of medical tourism will be given—from ancient Greece to the present-day medical hub of Dubai City. Finally, for readers to understand the multifaceted and multiplayer market of medical tourism and how these players engage with one another in the patient's treatment-seeking journey, the model of the four modes of medical tourism will be presented.

Definition: International and Intranational Medical Tourism

What is medical tourism? There is more than one definition depending on what context it refers to. Other synonymous terms used are medical travel, healthcare outsourcing, globalization of health care, and even health tourism. Regarding the flow of patients geographically, there is an import side and an export side to medical tourism. This book focuses on the import side of medical tourism—the outflow of domestic residents specifically from developed economies to seek medical, dental, and cosmetic surgeries from healthcare providers in developing economies. As a result, there is an outflow of revenues, for instance, from the United States to other countries, thus reducing the value of the gross domestic product (GDP) of the United States. The import side of medical tourism is a stark difference from the export side, wherein there is an influx of residents from less developed or developing countries to developed economies seeking medical treatments. In the United States, such has been the case until September 11, 2001. Once potential patients commit to traveling for care, they sometimes, though not always, visit some interesting sights in the destination country, therefore the term "medical tourism." This book focuses more on the "medical" than the "tourism" part, as the former is travel's primary and intended purpose.

Defined as "medical travel," it refers to anyone who travels a distance (either out of the country or out of their home states) to seek healing for their bodies. They do not necessarily engage in any form of tourism or sightseeing. On the other hand, "health tourism" is a broader concept embraced predominantly by the European Union. It involves natural and holistic treatments such as spas, thermal springs, yoga, massage, Ayurvedic medicine, and traditional Chinese medicine, including herbs and acupuncture. Many refer to such therapies as "wellness" in the United States. Many European economies embrace this broader concept to the point that their insurance companies reimburse these holistic approaches. A case in point is thermal treatments, which are well recognized in Italy and are included in the therapeutic program of its national health system (Gianfaldoni et al., 2017). Unfortunately, the insurance industry in the United States has not caught up with reimbursing treatments included in "health tourism," otherwise known as complementary and alternative medicine (CAM). It is comforting to know that the Food and Drug Administration (FDA) in the United States has recently approved chiropractic care and acupuncture as legitimate pain-management therapies since June 2020. These therapies are, therefore, now covered by most insurance companies.

Value and Growth of Medical Tourism

Regarding the value of global medical tourism, whether internationally or within the United States, various figures have been reported from different sources. According to one source, the global market was valued at $105 billion in 2019 and is projected to reach $274 billion by 2027 at a 12.8 percent compound annual growth rate (CAGR) between 2019 and 2027 (Allied Market Research, 2020). In terms of volume, 23 million had traveled worldwide in 2019, with expected growth to 70.3 million by 2027, with a 15 percent CAGR between 2019 and 2027. According to another source, the global medical tourism market was predicted to grow to $207 billion by 2027 (Matthews & Freund, 2022). The same source also stated that during the pre-pandemic year of 2019, an estimated 780,000 Americans traveled abroad for treatment, compared to 650,000 in 2021. The 2021 figure was an increase of 124 percent from 2020, which was at the beginning of the Covid-19 pandemic year.

Elsewhere outside the United States, as the Covid-19 pandemic of 2020–2 has eased in most parts of the world, medical tourism's growth has been phenomenal. In South Korea, the number of incoming medical tourists has jumped by approximately 70 percent, from 146,000 in 2021 to 248,000 in 2022 (Lee, 2023). Similarly, the number of medical tourists arriving in India has increased by 9.2 percent, from 595,000 in 2019 to 650,000 in 2022, a significant increase from the previous year (Naik, 2023). Dubai is considered one of the top medical tourism hubs in the world. In 2022, the city received 674,000 medical tourists (*Gulf Business*, 2023).

As the values and growth of medical tourism worldwide have demonstrated above, a similar trend is observed in the United States. In 2019 alone, it was reported that the number of Americans who traveled to Mexico for care was at least 1.2 million (O'Neil, 2023). We expect the outflow of Americans to medical tourism destinations besides Mexico to exceed a few million quickly. Healthcare spending in the United States grew by 2.7 percent to $4.3 trillion between 2021 and 2022, or 18.3 percent of GDP or $12,914 per person (Center for Medicare and Medicaid Services, 2022). As the cost of US health care continues to rise, as the third-party payers provide less coverage, as the household incomes rise and the population ages, and as there are increasingly vital government initiatives and support from destination economies, the US medical tourism industry is on its definite path to growth.

Historical Development

One can only fully understand the medical tourism industry by first delving into its history and development. The history of medical tourism dates back thousands of years before Christ, and it was widespread and practiced among different cultures of the world. The ancient Greeks were the first to travel to therapeutic temples, erected and honored after Asclepius, the Greek god of medicine (Health-tourism.com, 2022). Greek pilgrims traveled to these temples, one of the earliest healing centers, searching for a cure for their diseases. Epidaurus was one of the most well-known spa sanctuaries, and it included facilities like a gymnasium, a dream temple, and thermal baths. Other similar ones were the Sanctuary of Zeus in Olympia and the Temple of Delphi. Today, these ruins remain popular tourist spots for sightseeing. Even in India, dating back five thousand years ago, the popularity of yoga and Ayurvedic medicine has attracted travelers and spiritual students to flock to the country to seek alternative treatments (Health-tourism.com, 2022). The rise of the Roman Empire saw the emergence of thermae (hot water baths and springs) as popular commercial and social networking centers among the upper social class and as healing centers. During biblical times, in the Gospels of Saints Matthew, Mark, Luke, and John, Jesus was depicted as traveling with His disciples mostly on foot from place to place for miles to heal the sick. People in those days had to travel a long distance, sometimes by boat, to get to the miracle health provider, Jesus, to seek healing for their physical ailments.

In the sixteenth century, the upper social class revisited the Roman baths. It flocked to spa towns such as St. Mortiz in Switzerland, Ville d'Eaux in Italy, Aachen in Germany, and Bath in England (Health-tourism.com, 2022). In the eighteenth century, spa towns were considered early forms of medical tourism, so the Europeans visited spas due to the therapeutic mineral waters that were effective in treating ailments such as bronchitis, gout, and liver diseases (Gahlinger, 2008). Fast-forward to the 1980s and 1990s, the escalating healthcare cost again sparked new interest in seeking treatments offshore or abroad. Dental tourism was among the most popular in Central American countries such as Costa Rica, Mexico, and Cuba. Cuba has also attracted international patients for eye surgeries and cardiac and cosmetic procedures (Pickert, 2008).

The Asian financial crisis of 1997 and the collapse of Asian currencies were a catalyst for many Asian countries to redirect their tourism marketing efforts to include international healthcare services. Thailand soon became the hub for plastic surgery and other routine medical procedures. Incidentally, the Joint Commission International (JCI) was established in 1997 to accredit international healthcare facilities for compliance with international healthcare standards. The aftermath of September 11, 2001, and the real estate boom in Asia have seen the global medical tourism market grow to its all-time height. Southeast Asian countries such as Singapore, Malaysia, Thailand, India, and many Latin American countries quickly emerged as popular healthcare destinations. The trend can be attributed partly to the timely JCI accreditation of many of their hospitals and their strategic affiliation with well-known US medical centers such as Harvard Medical International, Johns Hopkins International, and the Cleveland Clinic.

Four Modes of Medical Tourism

While the historical account of medical tourism may be fascinating, today, the exponential growth of the global medical tourism industry in such a short time has propelled the market to evolve beyond a simple transaction between a patient and a foreign healthcare provider. Today, there are likely to be other third-party players such as facilitators, insurance companies, employers, and patient's domestic doctors involved in the transaction. In order to explain the multifaceted, multilevel industry, the author conceptualized the model of the four modes of medical tourism in 2009. The model describes the market transactions of four or five leading players who participate in the medical tourism market. Each of the four modes explains a unique way of achieving its treatment-seeking goal—from the patients to the final healthcare providers outside the country in most cases. Each mode can also explain a transactional journey between the buyers and sellers in this market, with the possible involvement of intermediaries such as the medical tourism facilitators (or agents) or patients' insurance companies or employers.

Simply put, the five key players in the marketplace of medical tourism are as follows:

1. Domestic patients
2. Medical tourism facilitators
3. Domestic insurance companies or employers
4. Domestic healthcare providers
5. Foreign healthcare providers

These players and their interactions with each other are illustrated in the four modes diagram in Figure 1. In mode 1, a domestic patient becomes aware of the availability of foreign healthcare providers (FHPs) and contacts them directly. Mode 2 is represented by the medical tourism facilitators (MTFs) and their support suppliers, such as travel insurance, financing, payment firms, air ambulance, and nursing services. Mode 3 represents insurers, employers, and support suppliers, such as medical-cost management consultants and risk-management consultants. Finally, mode 4 illustrates another channel in which patients are referred or encouraged to travel by their domestic healthcare providers.

Mode 1: Domestic Patients and Challenges

Mode 1 is the earliest and simplest form of medical tourism, from ancient Greek pilgrims traveling to Epidaurus to present-day Americans crossing the border to Mexico to get a dental implant. The patients in this mode are either familiar with the foreign healthcare providers in the destination country or have done their research. They are confident in arranging their medical procedures and traveling

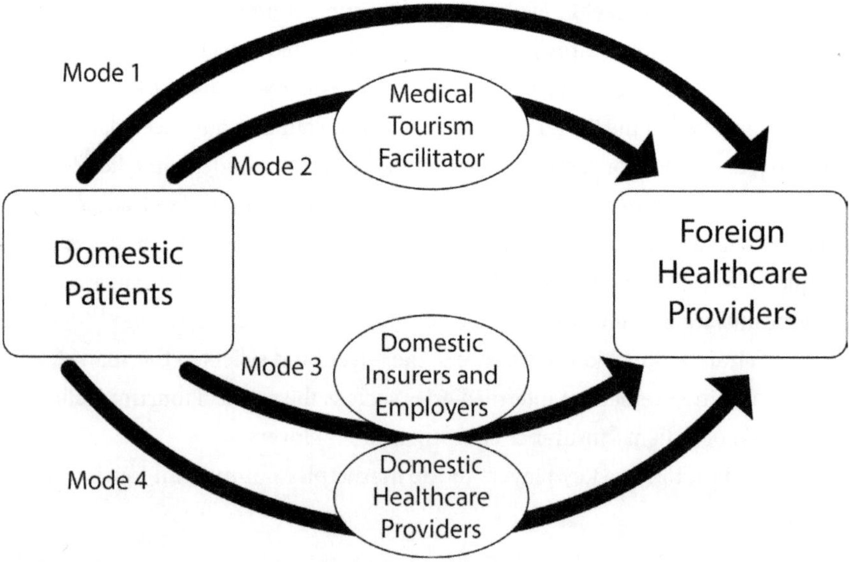

Figure 1 The four modes of medical tourism.

independently. Occasionally, they may employ the informal help of their families or friends who reside in the destination country to arrange travel and other procedures. In other instances, they may even contact the international patient centers of their destination facilities directly or less frequently using their home countries' offshore affiliated marketing offices if they are available. The patients in mode 1 typically consist of those with prior medical travel experience. They are likely to be underinsured and uninsured in developed economies. Preventive treatment such as routine physical examinations and dental procedures are commonly sought by patients in this mode, as well as cardiovascular, orthopedic, bariatric, and cosmetic surgeries.

As mentioned, many patients from mode 1 are experienced medical tourists who are uninsured and underinsured. One of the significant challenges they face is coming up with sufficient funds to cover both the medical procedure and the travel expenses to the destination country. For instance, a coronary artery bypass graft (CABG) surgery can cost from $45,000 to $448,000 (or a median price of $247,000) in the United States (Giacomino et al., 2016). It is typical for the middle-aged, middle-income uninsured in America to sell their homes to afford such surgery. Not all the patients in this mode are uninsured. The insured's concerns are whether their insurance coverage is portable across country borders so they may receive reimbursements from their insurance companies. Common sense dictates that one must check with one's insurance company before embarking on a costly medical journey. Cost savings is one of the main motivating forces that attract potential patients to travel for care. For the same CABG procedure, it would cost a median price of $24,000 in Mexico and $42,000 in Singapore; the cost saving is 90 percent and 83 percent, respectively, even after adding the minimal round-trip airfare ($800 to $1,800), the cost savings are still too hard to ignore. One can see medical tourism's strong pull in such significant cost savings.

However, since quality and continuity of care are legitimate concerns for most potential patients, could the difficulty of having the patient's domestic healthcare system deal with potential complications, side effects, and postoperative care be so significant that they outweigh the cost savings from medical tourism? For that matter, it is vitally important for patients in mode 1 to conduct their pre-trip research on the prospective healthcare providers. It is also not unusual for some well-known international hospitals and medical tourism facilitators (MTFs) to offer complication insurance through a third-party payer to potential patients to ensure their peace of mind. In addition, patients in mode 1 may want to study how the legal system in the destination country handles cases of medical negligence or malpractice. If something goes wrong, the potential litigation costs could outweigh the cost savings in the first place. It is recommended that patients in this mode do sufficient independent research to avoid some of the potential pitfalls.

Patients in mode 1 rely on their resources when selecting a destination country. Because actual traveling is a vital part of their journey to seek care, they would want to maximize their traveling experience. Because they may face cultural and language barriers when they travel, a country's social and cultural compatibility becomes an important determinant when choosing a destination country. They tend to choose a country that speaks their languages. They also tend to be experienced travelers who know how to overcome travel risks and handle the hassle of travel. Travel risk means taking extra precautionary safety measures when traveling outside the country. For instance, be aware that when taking a long flight, dehydration and immobility may cause one to suffer from deep vein thrombosis and pulmonary emboli—as the website of the American Medical Association likes to warn potential medical tourists. A practical solution would be getting an aisle seat so one can get up often, walk around, and wear compression socks to ensure good blood circulation. On the other hand, the hassle of travel involves travel planning such as airline and hotel reservations, visa application, leave application, airport transiting, and even packing for the trip. Making a checklist months ahead can make these tasks more manageable than they seem.

Patients in this mode are likely to face some ethical and moral issues. These issues can be cut both ways. The availability of highly sensitive treatments such as stem cell therapy, organ transplantation, surrogate pregnancy, and late-term abortion may encourage some to travel to seek such treatments. However, it may deter some from traveling to countries that uphold these bioethical legislations. Likewise, due to confidentiality, some patients may choose to travel abroad for treatments such as drug rehabilitation, plastic surgery, or sex change. On the other hand, the lack of compliance with the American HIPAA (Health Insurance Portability and Accountability Act) or privacy law in some countries may imply no guarantee of confidentiality protection, thus deterring some from traveling abroad for such care.

Mode 2: Medical Tourism Facilitators and Uncertainty

Mode 2 represents the journey of a domestic patient who employs the service of an agent known as a medical tourism facilitator (MTF). The primary responsibility of an MTF is to match the patient's medical needs with a foreign healthcare provider. Once matched, the MTF would perform the service of a middleman from start to finish. These services may include arranging medical procedures, air travel, visa applications, lodging during recuperation, and sightseeing in the destination country if requested. Patients in this mode will likely have no prior experience with medical travel. They are best described as uninsured or underinsured, middle-aged, and having a middle income. They are more inclined to seek CABG, joint replacements, bariatric or cosmetic surgeries, and dental surgeries, essentially elective procedures sought by most medical tourists.

Due to their lack of experience and knowledge, patients in mode 2 are more likely to face *asymmetric information* and experience a higher *search cost* than those in mode 1, ultimately encountering higher uncertainty. They are often faced with a time crunch and website information overloading. Even with a specific treatment in mind, the choice of healthcare providers and destination countries from the Internet can be overwhelming, let alone comparing the quality of care and costs across healthcare providers in various countries. Language barriers and unfamiliar communication will likely add another layer of frustration. For all these reasons, patients in mode 2 hire a facilitator or agent.

Although hiring an agent can add to the cost of medical tourism, most are still willing to pay for the service as they consider the benefits of doing so outweigh the costs. Some agents bundle their services and charge a fixed price, while others charge an add-on service fee accordingly. The all-inclusive cost typically covers medical expenses such as hospitalization, physician fees, prescription drugs, nursing care, therapy outside the hospital, round-trip airfares, and hotel expenses. Some charge a flat concierge fee of approximately $200–500 plus the treatment costs, and some charge a commission as a share of the service costs they arrange. In contrast, others receive finder's fees directly from international healthcare providers. Before committing to the agent's service, a potential patient should carefully enquire about what each package would entail.

Finding the right agent is altogether a different ball game. The facilitator's industry is currently unregulated. The market for facilitators in the United States needs to be more cohesive; the global Covid-19 pandemic of 2020–2 has caused many to fold their businesses. A website review of facilitators by the author in 2020 showed that out of the 173 companies in business in 2013, only 51 (or 33 percent) were still around after the pandemic started (Gan, 2020). Of the remaining 67 percent who did not survive, 67 percent of their original website domains were no longer available, 22 percent of them had put them up for sale, and 11 percent had switched to other businesses.

While the uncertainty surrounding the facilitator industry may discourage potential patients from using their services, the good news is that some organizations attempt to provide training and certifications to both facilitators and healthcare providers, both domestically and internationally. Among the notable ones is Global Healthcare Accreditation, a spin-off of the Medical Tourism Association, an industry-self-regulated but well-recognized organization. The facilitators also directly face competition from international hospitals. These hospitals often have their international patient centers or even have their own offshore marketing offices located in various developed countries. Some established facilitators partner with notable foreign healthcare providers or insurance companies to attract potential patients. Some studies also show that having a physician on staff can lend credibility to services provided by the agents, as physicians are well-qualified to advise potential patients on healthcare choices.

Mode 3: Third-Party Payers and Assurance

In mode 3, domestic patients are induced to travel for care outside their countries by their third-party payers, such as employers or insurance companies. The latter are required to meet ERISA (Employee Retirement Income Security Act) fiduciary duty as managers of the group plans. Some third-party payers have begun incentivizing their insured employees to seek foreign medical care to contain escalating healthcare costs. Likewise, many international hospitals, mostly JCI-accredited or US-affiliated hospitals, have been included in the network of providers by some managed-care health plans to cut costs. Patients in mode 3 are medically insured and are likely to be middle-income, middle-aged, and moderately educated. They are also more prone to seek popular elective treatments covered by their health plans but not cosmetic surgeries.

As early as 2008, as healthcare costs continued to soar, US third-party payers such as Blue Cross Blue Shield of South Carolina, Blue Shield and Health Net, Anthem Wellpoint, and United Group Programs began to develop new plans to reimburse offshore treatments. As mentioned earlier, sending a patient to Thailand or Singapore for CABG could save the employers or the insurers approximately $22,000 to $35,000. Moreover, legislation that favors medical tourism, such as West Virginia House Bill 4359 of 2006 and Colorado House Bill 1143 of 2007, would have given the third-party payers an additional incentive to endorse medical tourism. Under the first House Bill, state employees of West Virginia would be allowed to participate in offshore healthcare services. The benefits include treatment costs, air tickets, and lodging for the employee and a companion. All copayments and deductibles would be waived, and 20 percent of the cost savings would be returned to the employee as a rebate.

From the perspective of the potential patients in mode 3, they should check with their insurance companies about the entire benefits package and if their desired treatment will be covered. If covered, these benefits include waivers for deductibles and copayments, bonuses and rebates, paid leave, and airfares for the employee and a companion. They may even include travel and complications insurance as parts of the package or as riders. Furthermore, they should ensure that the destination countries and the international healthcare providers comply with information privacy policies such as the one required by HIPAA in the United States. The purpose of the act is to protect the patient's information and restrict the use and sharing of information.

Third-party payers face the complexity of dealing with an international billing system, which can include converting foreign exchanges and learning a different measurement standard, such as the metric system. To design a unique yet attractive plan, third-party payers may wish to outsource expertise such as legal service, risk management, software solutions, or partnering with an established facilitator.

Furthermore, and more importantly, potential patients look to their third-party payers for the assurance of quality of care and patient safety, as these are primarily the fiduciary responsibilities of third-party payers. While quality of care usually refers to quality assurance, control procedures, clinical practice, and facility operation, patient safety relates mainly to travel and surgical risks. It is difficult to compare the quality of care in domestic US hospitals with that of international hospitals. Some hospitals in the United States do not report surgical outcomes or participate in international performance measurement systems, as do many international hospitals outside the United States. Furthermore, there may be significant variations in treatment outcomes among accredited international hospitals, just as mortality and complication rates can vary among accredited hospitals within the same city in the United States.

As a side note, the Joint Commission International (JCI) and the World Health Organization (WHO) jointly developed international standards for patient safety in 2005. In addition to the JCI, other international accreditation standards are recognized outside the United States. These are the International Society for Quality in Healthcare (IsQua), QHA Trent Accreditation (formerly Trent Accreditation Scheme) (UK), Accreditation Canada (ACI), and Australian Council on Healthcare Standards (ACHS).

Currently, no law prevents international medical travel. The American Medical Association (AMA), American College of Surgeons (ACS), and American Dental Association (ADA) have all issued statements recognizing patients' rights to choose their physicians and hospitals. They all highlight the importance of post-care and their related financial responsibilities. ACS specifically supports the view that third-party payers should be responsible for coordinating and reimbursing post-care in the United States, including managing complications, readmission, rehabilitation, and long-term care.

Even with international accreditations of foreign healthcare providers and assurance of patient risk and safety on the part of the third-party sponsors, clinically or externally, there can never be 100 percent guaranteed, so there is the need to buy insurance. There is currently no health insurance regulation that covers medical tourism. All these may explain why many insurance companies are still hesitant to participate in medical tourism despite substantial cost savings.

Mode 4: Domestic Healthcare Providers and Promise

Mode 4 is the most uncommon mode of all the modes. Domestic patients in this mode experience the global healthcare transaction formally referred by their domestic healthcare providers. Though unusual, it is gaining popularity. This mode is an extension of domestic healthcare providers, mainly "big-name" prestigious hospitals, outsourcing their medical services to other countries. Many offshore hospitals actively participating in medical tourism are accredited by JCI. In addition, many of them are also affiliated with prestigious US hospitals such as Johns Hopkins International, Harvard Medical International, and Cleveland Clinic. Some US healthcare providers with international presence already share their management protocols with foreign hospitals. For instance, Johns Hopkins has established consulting and referral relationships with affiliated hospitals in Singapore, Turkey, and India. These arrangements generate revenues through fees and often result in international patient referrals.

Deloitte reported that 40 percent of US consumers would travel outside their immediate area to seek care for at least 50 percent savings if their doctors recommended it (Deloitte, 2009). Some patients may receive offshore care referred by their home doctors for various reasons. For instance, due to limited access to primary health care in their home countries, patients from countries bordering South Africa were referred by their doctors to South Africa (Crush & Chikanda, 2015). In other cases, Dutch doctors recommended their patients seek care at a nearer cross-border foreign facility (in Germany or Belgium) with a shorter wait list instead of at the closest Dutch facility (Brouwer et al., 2003). Further, it is common for doctors to travel to hospitals in another country to conduct surgeries. Holliday et al. (2015) reported, "South Korean doctors often perform consultations and surgeries in China; clinics in Spain host surgeons from Germany or Italy." Some itinerant US surgeons have traveled to perform surgeries in destination countries, even requiring patients to receive the entire care at those locations (Hery et al., 2023).

Regarding medical tourism, domestic doctors are often involved in pre-care and post-care directly or indirectly. The patients may undergo a pre-trip checkup and follow-up care with their domestic doctors upon returning home. Specific ethical and moral issues may arise throughout the patient's healing journey. They may come in the form of medical complications because of procedures performed by a foreign doctor and, subsequently, imposing an additional responsibility of a home doctor to care for the patient.

From an institutional perspective, those in favor of medical tourism make two points: (1) keeping the option of a lower-cost offshore healthcare alternative would allow Americans access to quality care; (2) it would also relieve the strain on public resources for the uninsured as procedures offered offshore become increasingly more affordable. From economic and social viewpoints, outsourcing elective health care will reduce the demand pressure in the domestic healthcare system and allow the latter to serve the urgent healthcare demand of aging baby boomers, for instance, in long-term care and quality of life in retirement homes. All these may result in greater collaboration between domestic and foreign healthcare providers through affiliation agreements or formal patient referrals. They are painting the picture of an incredible promise for potential patients in mode 4.

2

Medical Tourists

What do Steve McQueen and Ronald Reagan have in common besides the fact that they were once great movie stars? They were both considered medical tourists at some point in their lives. One of the key players in the medical tourism market is the consumer or the patient or medical tourist. They are the ones who travel outside their country of residence primarily to seek medical treatment. Tourism may be an option. Tourists who travel to another country for sightseeing and have suffered from any illnesses that require medical attention are not considered medical tourists because their primary purpose for traveling is purely tourism and not seeking healthcare services. Similarly, expats who work and reside in a foreign country visiting a foreign healthcare facility to care for their medical needs are not considered medical tourists.

Having just defined medical tourists, who they are, and who they are not, next in this chapter, we will outline the profile of medical tourists, followed by an examination of their motivations to engage in medical tourism. These motivating factors will be presented as country-specific or hospital-specific. They will also be explained in terms of "push" or "pull" factors. The push factors are mainly the global and the domestic institutional environments that encourage consumers to exit the county for care. The pull factors are primarily the healthcare environment or certain healthcare-related features in destination countries or hospitals that attract consumers to seek care.

The Profile of Medical Tourists

Early studies showed that average medical tourists were in their fifties, married with four in the family, moderately educated (with a bachelor's degree), and earning an annual household income of $41,000 in the 1980s (or $109,000 in 2023 figures) (Goodrich & Goodrich, 1987). Recent studies and research have further shown that potential medical tourists from the United States motivated by economic reasons to travel for care were likely to be uninsured and underinsured, middle-income earners, and middle-aged (Forgione & Smith, 2006; Gan & Frederick, 2013a).

In a more recent survey of 427 medical tourists who traveled to Mexico for care, the average tourist was around 64.5 years old and had an annual income between $25,001 and $50,000. Most (92 percent) were motivated by cost savings (Miller et al., 2020). The most common procedure sought was dental, and antibiotics were the most common drugs sought. Most of the participants also expressed their intention to make a repeat visit.

We assume the health status of an average medical tourist is either good or excellent, as most studies have found. Looking at it from another perspective, it is possible too that those with good or excellent health would have less need to contact their domestic doctors or insurance companies, let alone travel offshore for care. On the other hand, for cross-border health care, studies conducted in South Texas showed that those who self-rated themselves as being in poor health were more inclined to travel to Mexico frequently to use healthcare services (Su et al., 2011).

Some studies have found that foreign language proficiency positively correlates to traveling offshore for care. For instance, many studies demonstrated that Hispanic Americans with low English proficiency tended to travel to Mexico or other Latin American countries for care (Su et al., 2011). Language barriers can even become an impediment to seeking care in the United States, such as in the case of some South Korean immigrants, to the point that they prefer to travel to their native country for care, especially among those who are uninsured (Lee, Kearns & Friesen, 2010).

What Motivates Them to Travel?

A potential patient from a developed economy would choose to travel for care in an emerging or developing country for many reasons. These medical tourists are motivated by push and pull factors. On the supply side, we have the convenience of gathering information from the Internet, the availability of offshore skilled healthcare professionals, and the emergence of affordable telecommunication and air travel that fuel the engine of the globalization of health care. These are the so-called push factors.

In the United States, legislatures that favor medical tourism are the institutional push factors that drive medical tourism. Examples are the West Virginia and Colorado House Bills. Another institutional push factor is the inducements by the third-party payers (employers and insurance companies) in the form of bonuses and cash incentives. In an incredible landmark case of Blue Ridge Paper Products, Inc., the company supposedly offered one of its employees the option to perform elective surgery at a PPO-approved hospital in India. The package included the airfares of the employee and a companion, extra sick leave, and a bonus of $10,000 (Milstein & Smith, 2006). As a cost containment measure, some managed-care health plans have begun to include international hospitals within their network of providers. The Blue Cross Blue Shield of California had recently provided discounted plans for their subscribers to receive care in Mexico. Likewise, Blue Cross Blue Shield of South Carolina formed its first international partnership with Bumrungrad Hospital in Thailand in early 2009. All these push factors have made medical tourism more accessible to domestic patients.

On the other hand, the demand side or the pull factors that drive medical tourism stress primarily the significant cost savings. The presence of a high cost does not guarantee high quality, and a low cost does not always indicate low quality. There are various reasons foreign hospitals in developing countries can offer significant cost savings in their medical procedures and services. These economies generally have minimal involvement of third-party payers, therefore incurring lower bureaucratic and administrative fees. They also have less stringent regulatory environments, thus requiring lower malpractice insurance expenses or litigation costs. In addition, labor and training costs and pharmaceutical charges are lower than those in advanced economies.

For instance, a heart bypass surgery (CABG) that costs around $123,000 in the United States might only cost $8,639 (including medical costs, airfare, and hotel accommodation) in a high-tech hospital in India using Western-trained surgeons, which constitutes a 93 percent saving (see Table 1). Gastric bypass surgery in the United States can cost approximately $26,000. In contrast, it can be done for around $11,000 (all-inclusive) in India or Mexico, representing a saving of almost 60 percent.

Other studies have noted other pull factors that motivate US patients to seek offshore treatments, such as minimal wait time, more personalized care, availability of specific unusual procedures, or a desire for treatment confidentiality.

Table 1 Cost Comparison of Selected Treatments in Selected Countries

Procedures	USA	India	Thailand	South Korea	Mexico	Colombia	Ukraine	Jordan
CABG	123,000	7,000	17,188	NA	25,000	11,200	17,000	14,400
Spinal fusion	110,000	12,000	9,500	23,000	16,000	27,000	3,000	NA
Hip replacement	40,364	10,500	7,813	25,000	13,500	8,000	4,000	6,345
Knee replacement	35,000	9,000	9,531	20,000	12,500	8,000	4,000	4,935
Gastric bypass	26,000	9,000	16,800	20,000	8,000	7,000	5,500	5,150
Facelift	11,000	7,200	2,813	6,000	6,200	5200	4,050	NA

Source: https://www.medicaltourism.com/compare-prices

Note: Most prices are median prices quoted from the year 2021.

Destination-Specific Factors

At the macro level, when selecting a particular country destination by potential patients, some country-specific pull factors they may consider are geopolitical concerns, social and cultural compatibility, whether a country is free from disasters, and its infrastructure. Some may even consider the bioethical legislations of a destination country, such as whether they offer stem cells, fertility treatment, and organ transplants.

At the destination hospital level, key pull factors that attract patients evolve mostly around the quality-of-care matrix. They can be summarized as follows: (1) international accreditation and reputation, (2) quality of care in terms of surgical outcomes and low nurse–patient ratio, (3) credentials and training of foreign doctors, (4) advanced medical technology and equipment, and (5) HIPAA compliance. For instance, in a Jordan hospital, a private hospital accredited by both the Joint Commission International (JCI) and the International Society for Quality (ISQua) in health care, most of their doctors receive their training in the United States, UK, Europe, and Canada. I have also visited a private hospital in Jordan with three resident MRI machines in one hospital alone, compared to one MRI machine shared by a few area hospitals in rural North Carolina, where I live. These offshore medical tourism hospitals are usually backed by state-of-the-art medical technology, equipment, and sophisticated research infrastructures. India, for instance, is one of the world's leading centers in biotechnology.

Other studies show that more hospital-specific pull factors such as the hospital's location (e.g., urban versus rural, distance from the airport), amenities (e.g., proximity to shopping, dining, and banking services), special diet (e.g., vegetarian, kosher, halal), and even the staff's attitude are essential in the decision-making process of the medical tourists.

Cost Saving

Cost saving is the strongest and the most cited motivation or pull factor for medical tourists to travel for care. A glance at Table 1 will explain why this is so. According to the figures in the table, an American can save 74 percent by getting a facelift in Thailand, a saving of 90 percent if they get a hip replacement done in Ukraine, or a whopping saving of 94 percent by having a CABG performed in India.

Inducement of Third-Party Sponsors

In addition to the unusual historic case of Blue Ridge Paper Products, Inc., mentioned earlier, as healthcare costs continued to rise in the 1980s, US third-party payers such as United Group Programs, Inc., Anthem Wellpoint, Blue Shield and Health Net, and Blue Cross Blue Shield of South Carolina began to innovate by reimbursing treatments received by domestic patients abroad. Furthermore, if passed, pro-medical tourism houses bills such as those in West Virginia and Colorado would have given employers and insurance companies additional incentives to offer medical tourism. For instance, the West Virginia House Bill would have allowed state employees to travel abroad and paid for treatment, air transportation, and accommodations for the employee and a companion, with a 100 percent waiver for copayments and deductibles. All these are push factors that will encourage domestic patients to travel offshore for treatments.

Minimal Wait List

The traditional universal healthcare systems, such as the National Health Service (NHS) in the United Kingdom and Canada, are notorious for long wait lines for significant procedures. Nearly 40 percent of NHS hospital departments in England have an average treatment wait time of more than eighteen weeks, with some treatments well over thirty weeks (Jayanetti, 2022). Many of the most delayed non-cancer specialties came from hospitals performing orthopedics (nearly 67 percent), spinal surgery (80 percent), and upper gastrointestinal surgery (70 percent). The delays were attributed to the post-Covid-19 pandemic of 2020–2 pent-up demand and the challenges faced by the NHS in delivering care, primarily due to insufficient beds and staff.

Patients in developed economies generally do not tolerate such delays well. As we know, delayed treatment can cause patients' health to deteriorate, and those who suffer severe pain may lose their mobility or their ability to work. Some may increasingly require more potent painkillers and may eventually lose their independence. All these will add additional burdens to the domestic healthcare systems. In the case of patients in Denmark who had to wait six months for orthopedic surgeries, 60 percent had already chosen to travel to hospitals outside the country with shorter waiting times. Based on this factor alone, many more patients in developed economies who could not put up with delayed treatments had turned to offshore hospitals as their only option.

In many destination hospitals in countries such as Singapore, Malaysia, and Thailand, depending on the types of medical procedures, appointments for standard surgical procedures can be scheduled within a week or two, sometimes even within days. Many medical tourism destination hospitals are willing to accommodate medical travelers, knowing they have limited time to spend in the destination countries.

For some patients who experience long wait times, the trade-off becomes traveling a longer distance versus a longer wait time. A study evaluating patients' choices in London found that for every additional hour of travel, on average, patients would require a reduction in wait time of 2.1 months to elicit them to travel for care in an offshore healthcare facility (Burge et al., 2005).

Similarly, the Fraser Institute in Canada reported a median wait time of 27.4 weeks (approximately seven months) between referral from a family doctor to a specialist, the consultation with the specialist, and, eventually, the treatment or surgery itself. This figure was longer than the 20.9 weeks the pre-Covid-19 figure reported in 2019 (Moir & Barua, 2022). The median waitlist between a primary care doctor's referral and the actual procedure was the longest for neurosurgery (fifty-nine weeks), orthopedic surgeries (forty-eight weeks), and ophthalmology (thirty-five weeks). The shortest waits came from oncology-related services, elective cardiovascular surgery, and internal medicine, ranging from 3.7 to 18.7 weeks. Although these figures may be lower than those reported in the NHS in England, they are still considered high by developed economics standards. It is no wonder that many turn to medical tourism as their only solution.

The United States needs to be fairing better regarding wait time to see a physician. A recent US survey in 2022 shows that the average wait time to see a doctor in five specialties was twenty-six days in fifteen of the largest cities (Miller, 2022). When scheduling an appointment for elective surgeries such as orthopedics, the wait time was seventeen days, followed by twenty-one days in family medicine, twenty-seven days in cardiology, thirty-one days in obstetrics and gynecology, and thirty-five days in dermatology. While these wait times seem shorter than those in the UK or Canada, they are still considered intolerable by American standards if timely treatments are needed.

More Personalized Care

In many destination hospitals, the physicians are often assisted by more nurses per person than any facility the advanced economies could offer. Some facilities provide single-patient rooms resembling a five-star hotel suite more than a traditional hospital one. Some of these rooms come with one-on-one nursing care twenty-four hours a day. The rooms sometimes have high-speed Internet services and often even an extra bed for the companion.

A typical patient perceives the quality of care at the hospital level as more personalized and attentive. Other areas can include the good credentials of the doctors, the facility's reputation, advanced medical equipment and technology, amenities and food offered, facility cleanliness, compliance with HIPAA standards, and assurance of postoperative care. All these areas of quality of care together form a strong matrix of pull factors for a medical tourist to travel offshore for care.

Unavailability of Treatments in the Home Country

The unavailability of treatment in the home country of medical tourists is another critical driver pushing them to travel for care. This factor can be considered a push or a pull factor. The treatments sought can either be treatments approved by medical tourists' home countries, or they can be non-approved remedies such as stem cell therapies, organ transplants, fertility treatment, and abortion. The push factor is closely linked to approved procedures unavailable in some medical tourists' home states or countries. The pull factor is one reason some medical tourists would travel to access the list of non-approved treatments unavailable in their native states or countries.

Let us explore the category of push factors motivated by the unavailability of "approved treatments" first. There are plenty of examples worldwide. For instance, in many less developed economies in southern parts of Africa, due to a general lack of access to primary health care at home, many have crossed the borders to seek medical help in both the border towns and the major cities in South Africa (Crush & Chikanda, 2015). The majority of them did that because the procedures they sought after were not being offered in their home countries. Others were referred by their domestic healthcare providers to healthcare facilities in South Africa.

Similarly, the inadequate healthcare system in Laos has "pushed" Laotians to cross the borders to seek better care in Thailand. In this case, the social networks surrounding potential patients are a key push factor (Bochaton, 2015). Even though one may have limited income and knowledge of geography, being part of an active and extended social network has allowed one to travel to Thailand for care. The "spatial knowledge" effect also contributes toward making cross-border travel for care possible here—as many patients often travel to Thailand for business, shopping, sightseeing, or visiting family, making good use of their spatial knowledge.

During the Covid-19 pandemic between 2020 and 2021, except for a brief period of temporary closure due to the "peaks" in the number of Covid-19 cases, Turkey's medical tourism destination hospitals mainly stayed open. Most of their international patients came from emerging or less developed economies such as Russia, Romania, Bulgaria, Azerbaijan, Serbia, East Africa, and Arabic-speaking countries. These patients traveled for lifesaving emergency treatment because, as one hospital source put it, "they either travel or they will die." Essentially, they did not have any option not to travel for treatment. Fortunately, the Turkish Ministry of Health allowed transportation by car from other countries through the borders for medical surgeries. However, prior authorization was required, and patients and their companions had to be subject to the regular quarantine routines during the pandemic.

Moving on to the pull factors motivated by the availability of "non-approved treatments" in destination countries but unapproved in the medical tourists' native countries. Examples mentioned earlier include stem cell therapies, organ transplants, fertility treatment, and abortion. Most of these treatments are controversial and involve specific ethical and safety issues. We will discuss these in more detail in Chapters 6 and 9.

Stem Cell Therapies

Regarding stem cell therapies, countries like the United States have stricter regulations from the Food and Drug Administration (FDA) than others. "Stem cell tourism" is popular in destination countries such as China, India, Thailand, Mexico, Costa Rica, the Caribbean, Latin America, and former Soviet Union countries. Stem cell therapies can be used to treat various serious diseases such as Alzheimer's, auto-immune disease, burns, cancer, heart disease, osteoarthritis, orthopedics, Parkinson's disease, sclerosis, spinal cord injuries, stroke, and type 1 diabetes, to name just a few. However, most of these therapies are not approved by the FDA in the United States, although clinical trials have been conducted in various US institutions. According to the Harvard Stem Cell Institute, "the only stem cell therapies that have been proven safe and effective are those constituting what is known as bone marrow transplantation for treatment of some cancers" (Harvard Stem Cell Institute, 2023).

Reproductive Tourism

One of the more controversial forms of medical tourism is reproductive tourism, more appropriately termed "reproductive travel." According to a report, approximately 17.5 percent of the adult population worldwide, or one in six, will experience infertility during their reproductive lives (World Health Organization, 2023). Seeking offshore assisted reproductive treatments has been on the rise, and this can take many forms. They can range from in-vitro fertilization (IVF) treatment, surrogacy, donor eggs or donor sperm, and even gender selection.

Due to certain regulatory restrictions that prevent couples from accessing the desired services in their native countries, crossing the border to access assisted reproductive treatment may be their only viable option to have children. Some may travel due to their legal ineligibility; for instance, they may be unmarried or in a same-sex relationship due to their failure to meet the age eligibility for state-subsidized care or simply the couples' inability to produce eggs or sperm. Some may travel because of a preference for donor anonymity. In contrast, others want more information or choices when selecting a donor, which may be prohibited in their home countries. Due to religious, ethical, or legislative restrictions, different countries offer or restrict specific fertility procedures. While commercial surrogacy and ova donation are banned in most of the European Union, Australia, Canada, and Japan, they are considered legal in India and some states in the United States. The United States itself is regarded as a destination country for commercial surrogacy or gender selection.

Countries that have become major hubs for reproductive services are Belgium, Czech Republic, Spain, and North Cyprus in Europe; Israel, Jordan, South Africa, and the United Arab Emirates in the MENA region; Argentina and Mexico in Central and South America; and India and Thailand in Asia. The Czech Republic and Spain have been known for ample supplies of donor eggs, and India for low-cost commercial surrogacy.

Organ Transplants

In the United States, approximately 46,000 organ transplants were performed in 2023. Out of the total, many of them involved kidney (63 percent) and liver (24 percent) (Organdonor.gov, 2024). At this writing, at least 103,223 Americans are on the waitlist for organ transplants. On average, while a new name is added to the list every ten minutes, seventeen people die daily waiting for an organ to become available. These are stark statistics and a classic example of demand that far exceeds supply, resulting in shortages of organs.

To circumvent the shortages, many desperate patients resort to traveling offshore to procure an organ, hence the term "transplant tourism." Transplant tourism is a highly controversial area of medical tourism as it sometimes involves trading organs on the "black market," making it legally or ethically wrong (Whitlock, 2022). According to early WHO data, up to 10 percent of global transplants involve patients who travel outside their countries to buy an organ (Shimazono, 2007).

Iran and Saudi Arabia are the only countries that legalize the trading of organs in this writing. In the 1990s, there were reports on travel for commercial organ transplantations in regions such as South Africa, South America, and the Indian subcontinents. At its peak, China, which is known to perform more international transplants than any other country, was widely believed to obtain organs from executed prisoners who were sold to international patients, representing at least 5,000 potential cases annually (Budiani-Saberi & Delmonico, 2008). Most transplant travelers acquire organs from living vendors in Colombia, India, Pakistan, and the Philippines.

Some of the significant issues surrounding transplant tourism involve the living donors. For instance, in India, they are often promised a large sum of money in exchange for their organ donation, which is usually a scam, and the donors end up not getting paid. Since selling an organ is considered illegal in most countries, including India, there is no recourse for the potential donor (Whitlock, 2022). As far as the surgery outcome is concerned, often, less care is taken to match the donor and recipient, resulting in a higher level of rejection and a greater risk of death. Further, if surgical complications arise, domestic doctors are often unwilling to care for a patient who circumvents the donor process in the United States to obtain their transplant from an unknown source outside the country.

Greater Privacy and Confidentiality

When a potential patient desires greater privacy and confidentiality in treatment, there is no better place to go than outside the country. That explains why cosmetic and bariatric surgeries are popularly sought across the border in Mexico or outside the United States—in many Latin American countries such as Brazil, Peru, and Panama. Gender reassignment or sex change is another procedure that a potential patient would value greater confidentiality. It is no wonder that it is a growing niche in the medical tourism industry in Thailand, attracting as many as two million medical tourists annually.

Reproductive tourism can be considered a highly confidential treatment as we often do not know the motives and reasons behind individuals seeking such treatment. In the case of pop singer Michael Jackson, he allegedly asked for several sperm donors. Eventually, he selected Mark Lester, formerly a child actor from the UK, who played the title role in the musical Oliver!, as the biological father of his first two children. Subsequently, his third, supposedly his only biological child, was conceived from a surrogate mother in Mexico. We know very little about the origin of the mother; all we know is that her privacy is being protected, presumably for legal reasons.

Alternative or Traditional Remedies

Nevertheless, some medical tourists travel offshore to seek alternative and traditional remedies such as Ayurvedic, yoga, massage, relaxation, and meditation. Many such therapies require relaxation techniques, usually sought at a spa town or near the mountains. For instance, meditations are often sought in remote high-altitude mountain ranges of Tibet, just as white sand beaches along the shores of the Carolinas are well-sought spots for morning yoga sessions.

In addition, Mexico has been another hotbed in alternative cancer treatment. For decades, celebrities have traveled across the border to seek FDA-unapproved alternative therapies, mostly natural or holistic, in treating cancer. Famous people like Coretta Scott King (Martin Luther King, Jr.'s wife) and movie star Steve McQueen have traveled to Mexico for alternative treatments for cancer in the last few decades. It is common knowledge that President Reagan had colon cancer and was operated on in the United States in 1985. He later received laetrile infusion for thirteen months from an unknown source when the therapy was unapproved by the FDA (and it is still unapproved today) but was obtainable outside the United States. Subsequently, Reagan traveled to Germany to seek natural cancer treatment from a German doctor. He lived another eighteen years and passed away at age ninety-three, not from cancer but from Alzheimer's disease in 2004.

Vacationing

In any literature or studies relating to medical tourism, we often see more emphasis on the "medical" aspect rather than the "tourism" aspect. Tourism or sightseeing opportunities are usually the secondary reason for traveling offshore in this context. However, when choosing a destination country for elective surgery, such as a cosmetic or bariatric operation, specific sightseeing opportunities offered by the same country may be as crucial as selecting healthcare providers. After all, if one is already in the host country, before or after the procedures, if conditions allow, why not relax, take a vacation, and take in some sights? That by itself may contribute positively to one's healing process.

The marketing department or tourism board of the destination countries indeed knows how to maximize the experiences of medical tourists. When the medical tourism industry reached its peak around the mid-2000s, it was common to hear or read marketing or promotional phrases such as "club medic," "sun, surf, surgery," and "surgeon and safari." While getting a "knee resurfacing," a less invasive procedure with a shorter recovery time than "knee replacement" in India, one can take the opportunity to visit the world-famous Taj Mahal or White Tiger National Park. While getting dental work or a facelift in Costa Rica, one can enjoy a wide range of biodiversity and ecotourism in its lush tropical jungle, including a zip line through the jungle! One can enjoy a donkey ride in Petra or a dip in the Dead Sea while getting an elective surgery or wellness check done at healthcare facilities in Jordan or Israel.

Cultural Similarity

Cultural similarity is another essential consideration when choosing which country to travel to for care. Cultural similarity can include a familiar care environment or the fluency with which the patient's native language is spoken by hospital staff. Muslim medical tourists from the Middle East, for instance, may choose to travel to Malaysia instead of Thailand since "halal" food is readily available, including in healthcare facilities in Malaysia. Regarding cultural compatibility, for instance, it is understandable that Jordan attracts Arabic-speaking medical tourists from Palestine, Iraq, Syria, and other Gulf Council Countries (GCCs), including Bahrain, Kuwait, Oman, Qatar, Saudi Arabia, and the United Arab Emirates. Among the medical tourists who arrived in South Korea in 2022, the United States accounted for the most significant percentage, followed by China (36 percent together with the United States), Japan (8.8 percent), Thailand (8.2 percent), and Vietnam (Lee, 2023). Except for the United States, it is noted that a good proportion of the medical tourists in South Korea came from neighboring countries with similar cultures.

3

Treatment Types

After reviewing the profile of medical tourists and their motivations in the previous chapter, we are ready to define the products and services medical tourists purchase in the medical tourism market and throughout their healing journeys. For the most part, medical tourism involves elective treatment, not emergency treatment requiring immediate lifesaving attention. Although there are cases in which cross-border air ambulances or private jets are used for emergency purposes, they are not the norm.

We will begin by covering common offshore elective treatments typical medical tourists seek. These treatments may be categorized as follows:

1. Medical (e.g., joint replacement, spinal fusion)
2. Bariatric or weight-loss procedures (e.g., gastric sleeve, tummy tuck)
3. Cosmetic or plastic surgery (e.g., facelift, liposuction)
4. Dental (e.g., crowns, implants, and root canals)
5. Vision (e.g., Cataract, LASIK)

Since cancer is the second most prevalent cause of death and a fast-growing disease in the United States, and our readers may have families or loved ones who are affected by it, we will devote a section on complementary and alternative medicine with a particular emphasis on holistic ways of treating cancer both domestically and internationally.

Elective Treatment

An elective treatment can typically be classified as "medically necessary" or cosmetic. This differentiation is essential mainly from the perspective of insurance reimbursement. Most third-party payers will pay for medically necessary procedures such as coronary artery bypass graft (CABG), joint replacements, or spinal fusion. Still, they may not cover cosmetic surgeries such as facelifts, liposuction, or tummy tuck.

There can be some gray areas regarding insurance reimbursement for bariatric treatment. Examples of bariatric treatment are weight loss surgeries such as gastric bypass, gastric sleeve, or tummy tuck. Bariatric treatments may be good options for those with obesity and those who have struggled with losing weight repeatedly, as well as for those who have type 2 diabetes. The trouble is that some insurance companies may treat bariatric treatment as medically necessary and, therefore, reimbursable. In contrast, others may view it as purely cosmetic and will bill their subscribers for the total cost.

Michael Jackson, the king of pop, is an excellent example of such gray areas. When he broke his nose and fell flat on the stage during one of his performances in 1979, that would be considered a medically necessary procedure to fix his nose. Subsequently, he had rhinoplasty done. It was then hard to determine whether the subsequent procedures restored the earlier nose injury or whether they were cosmetic to make his voice appear more high-pitched to appeal to his audience.

Medically Necessary Procedures

Before the growth of medical tourism peaked in the 2000s, most American medical tourists who had traveled abroad did so primarily to seek cosmetic surgeries. However, times have changed. Today, an increasing number of medical tourists who travel offshore for care seek mainly medically necessary treatments or "big ticket items" other than cosmetic surgeries.

Table 2 lists popular medically necessary procedures and cosmetic surgeries that medical tourists seek. As can be seen, the medically necessary procedures are mostly big ticket items compared to cosmetic surgeries. The higher cost of medically necessary treatments may explain why so many are motivated by cost-saving to travel offshore for care. Moreover, as shown in Table 2, bariatric surgeries such as gastric bypass, gastric sleeve, or lap band can cost $14,000 to $26,000 in the United States, so if the insurance companies do not cover these surgeries, US patients would have a solid motivation to travel offshore to receive these treatments for a fraction of the cost.

Cosmetic Surgeries

Cosmetic surgeries are medical procedures performed to improve the appearance of the body. Common examples of cosmetic surgeries are facelifts, rhinoplasty,

Table 2 Cost Comparison of Medically Necessary Procedures versus. Cosmetic Procedures

Medically necessary procedure	Median price ($) in USA	Cosmetic procedure	Median price ($) in USA
Heart valve replacement	170,000	Gastric bypass	26,000
CABG	123,000	Gastric sleeve	16,500
Spinal fusion	110,000	Lap band	14,000
Hip replacement	40,364	Facelift	11,000
Knee replacement	35,000	Tummy tuck	8,000
Angioplasty	28,200	Rhinoplasty	7,500
Hip resurfacing	28,000	Breast implants	6,400
IVF treatment	15,400	Liposuction	4,700
Hysterectomy	5,200	Dental implant	1,500

Source: https://www.medicaltourism.com/compare-prices.

or liposuction. In 2023, the top five cosmetic surgeries were liposuction, breast augmentation, tummy tuck, breast lift, and eyelid surgery. With the advancement of medical technology, the method chosen for cosmetic procedures has shifted from traditional open surgery to less invasive techniques. For instance, instead of going for a traditional facelift, one can opt for less invasive procedures such as injectables (or fillers), skin resurfacing using chemical peeling, skin abrasion or laser techniques, and tissue lifting.

Cosmetic surgery is by far the most popular type of procedure that are referred by medical tourism agents. Frederick and Gan (2015) found that 82 percent of 173 agents' websites they study advertised cosmetic surgeries. A liposuction costs an average of 4,700 in the United States. In 2023, there were 348,000 cases of liposuction performed in the Unites States, 93 percent of the liposuction procedures were sought by females, and 71 percent of the procedures were sought by those between thirty and fifty-four years old (American Society of Plastic Surgeons, 2023).

Cosmetic Dentistry

It is said that most dental surgeries are cosmetic. However, there is a clear distinction between general dentistry and cosmetic dentistry. General dentistry stresses preventive and restorative care, such as teeth cleanings, fillings, crowns, and bridges. On the other hand, cosmetic dentistry deals with aesthetics, such as a symmetrical and pleasing smile. Cosmetic dentistry includes teeth whitening,

Table 3 Cost Comparison of Dental Procedures between US and Mexico

	USA (in $)	Mexico (in $)
Basic cleaning	140	60
Simple tooth extraction	75–250	60–70
Surgical tooth extraction	180–420	150–90
Composite filling	90–250	65–125
Veneer	1,100–250	210–350
Crown	1,150–4,000	200–1,600
Dentures	1,800	300
Dental implant	1,800–3,900	750–1,500
Braces	5,500–13,000	2,000–4,500

Sources: Compiled by author, 2023.

dental bonding, veneers, and tooth and gum contouring. Since cosmetic dentistry procedures are usually nonessential from the health perspective, insurance companies typically do not cover them. Some procedures may fall into the gray area between general and cosmetic dentistry. For instance, braces can be considered a cosmetic procedure if the patients are conscious about their teeth and wish to improve their smiles. On the other hand, if a dental problem requires correction for oral health improvement, it is considered a medically necessary procedure reimbursable by most dental health plans.

Table 3 shows a cost comparison of some standard dental procedures between the United States and Mexico. Braces are one of the most common dental procedures sought by teenagers. The price range for this procedure available in Mexico is approximately three times lower than that in the United States. With such a substantial deep discount, it is no wonder dental tourism is among the most popular procedures among US medical tourists, especially for those without dental insurance. Mexico and Costa Rica are the most popular destinations among Americans for dental procedures.

Complementary and Alternative Medicine

There are often misconceptions about "complementary" and "alternative" medicine. The word complementary suggests working together to provide patients with the best alternatives, complementing each other's needs or offsetting each other's deficiencies. Complementary medicine, in this regard, means working in conjunction with mainstream or conventional medicine. It provides a holistic model of care for the body, spirit, and mind. Alternative medicine, on the other hand, implies a choice between two competing alternatives. Alternative medicine sometimes appears to promote "substitute" treatments for standard mainstream treatments for conditions such as cancer or other serious illnesses. The "competing" view may impact patients negatively as they invariably may benefit from both types of treatments, not just one or the other. A good example is the use of acupuncture to alleviate the side effects related to conventional chemotherapy undergone by cancer patients. Acupuncture is also known to help when combined with physical therapy for rehabilitation from an injury or surgery.

The tradition of natural medicine dates back several centuries, with an impressive worldwide accumulation of practical knowledge. The natural healing methods adopted by those with a holistic view of medicine aim to bring harmony and overall well-being. Interestingly, "health" is closely linked to wholeness and healing. In the last several decades, there has been a renewed interest in natural therapies widely known today as complementary and alternative medicine (CAM for short). According to a US study in 2017, about 38 percent of adults (eighteen years or older) and 12 percent of children (seventeen years or younger) are using some form of CAM, with the highest percentage being 44 percent among those in their fifties, and 36 percent among the young adults (eighteen–twenty-nine years) (National Center for Complementary and Alternative Medicine, 2018). Increasingly, there has been a recognition of its remarkable value as well as a shift away from some of the side effects and impersonal approaches of allopathic medicine (aka biomedicine, conventional medicine, mainstream medicine, orthodox medicine, and Western medicine), sometimes referred to as holding a "reductionist" view. Conventional medicine utilizes mainstream medical practices such as prescription drugs, diagnostic blood work, and surgery. CAM generally includes naturopathy, homeopathy, herbalism, and aromatherapy.

Naturopathy and Homeopathy

In a nutshell, naturopathy is applying common sense to health. The human body can heal itself, and the immune system will always attempt to overcome illness and restore balance. These attempts refer to using natural means such as diet, exercise, fresh air, relaxation, and even water use. The focus of naturopathy is, by and large, shifting the health responsibility back to patients themselves, and it stresses prevention rather than cure. Sickness is caused by environmental factors such as pollution and water intake quality. Naturopathy advocates many self-help actions. The main form of dietary treatment, for instance, is fresh and unprocessed foods, at times with emphasis on organic foods, and supported by the intake of supplements. Exercise is the most basic form of self-help, emphasizing good posture, correct breathing, adequate rest, and relaxation.

Homeopathy is widely acknowledged as an alternative form of medicine. Symptoms being treated are seen as part of the body's healing response to resist an illness instead of the adverse effects of sickness. Unlike conventional medicine, homeopathic remedies usually consist of natural substances prepared uniquely and prescribed in tiny amounts to restore health in the patient's self-healing process. Conventional medicine and homeopathy work well together. A study found that adding homeopathy improved survival and quality of life in patients with non-small cell lung cancer (NSCLC) (Frass et al., 2020). Despite working well with conventional medicine, homeopathic medicine is less prevalent in the United States than in major European countries such as Britain, France, Germany, and the Netherlands, where it is practiced by 20–50 percent of the doctors.

Herbalism and Aromatherapy

Ayurveda, the ancient Indian medical system, is based on a natural and holistic physical and mental health approach. Ayurvedic treatment combines diet, exercise, lifestyle, and products derived from plants but sometimes also from animals, minerals, and metals. Ayurveda is often associated with yoga, meditation, massage, and energy medicine.

Another oldest medical system is the traditional Chinese medicine (TCM), which dates back at least 2,200 years. Its goal is to prevent or cure disease by maintaining or restoring the balance of the human body's two complementary forces, *yin* and *yang*, thereby optimizing an individual's health. However, an imbalance of *yin* and *yang* will lead to sickness. To restore harmony, a range of traditional remedies such as acupuncture, acupressure, moxibustion, or cupping may be prescribed by the TCM practitioners. A brew of herbal "teas" may also be prescribed with combinations of medicinal plants or dried animal parts (e.g., insects, deer antlers, snakes, scorpions). The plant materials may include algae, barks, fern, flowers, fungus, lichen, moss, plants, seaweed, shrubs, or trees. Herbs may be prepared as infusions by soaking them in a liquid or decorating them—simmered in water over low heat for a certain period. In TCM, it is thought that different foods have different energies that can go directly to specific organs to help them heal. "Tai Chi" or "Qigong" are often associated with TCM. These ancient breathing exercises were developed to boost body, mind, and spirit energy, promoting overall health and well-being.

Natural Cancer Treatment

Historically, the use of complementary and alternative medicine (CAM) has been very successful in treating chronic diseases such as autoimmune conditions, cancer, diabetes, heart disease, and depression, to name a few. In the United States, cancer is the second leading cause of death next to heart disease, and its prevalence is rising quickly, especially in breast and prostate cancer. Some healthcare researchers predict it will soon catch up with heart disease to be the number one killer disease in the United States in the coming decades. Many natural or holistic approaches to treating cancer are being practiced worldwide. According to figures from 1981 to 2019, more than 50 percent of anticancer drugs originate from, or are derived from, natural products (Newman & Cragg, 2020). The remaining chapter will discuss some of these proven and evidence-based natural therapies for cancer treatment. This section does not attempt to be exhaustive in its coverage but rather represents some of the most effective modalities in holistic cancer treatment, either as a stand-alone therapy or sometimes in conjunction with conventional medicine. Some of these therapies may be available in the United States, as they are permissible by the Food and Drug Administration (FDA) and interstate law. However, most are only available outside the United States. Globally, a significant number of cancer patients utilize CAM in addition to conventional treatment.

Immunotherapy

Immunotherapy involves immunizing the patient with tumor cells or cell extracts, either by itself or in conjunction with an immune-stimulating vaccine. There are two types of active immunizations: (1) *allogeneic*, which uses someone else's cancer cells, and (2) *autologous*, which uses the cells of the patient himself. The pharmaceutical industry today favors the first type of vaccines because they can be quickly bottled and thus qualify as a standardized and marketable "one-size-fits-all" treatment. However, the second type of vaccine is more effective since it targets the patient's unique tumor. Still, it requires injecting cells into the patient. Although the National Institute of Health (NIH) has had about fifty clinical trials with autologous vaccines, they need a stringent protocol for patients to qualify for one of these trials. In short, for the most part US patients must travel to certain offshore health facilities, such as those in Germany or Mexico, to receive the autologous vaccine.

A famous success story of using immunotherapy is the oldest living former US President Jimmy Carter, who turned 100 years old in October 2024. When he was ninety years old, he was diagnosed with melanoma cancer that had spread to his brain; he was treated with Keytruda® (scientific name is pembrolizumab), a type of immunotherapy called checkpoint inhibitor that stimulates the body's immune system to detect and fight cancer cells. Many believed that by receiving this immunotherapy, Carter's life was extended by several years. In 2021, this world's top-selling cancer medication alone has generated a sale of $17 billion for Merck & Co., its sole manufacturer. Keytruda® is currently used to treat at least sixteen types of cancer, notably small cell lung cancer (SCLC). It is used by itself or with other treatments. As good as it sounds, however, Keytruda® comes with a hefty price tag. As of March 2024, the list price for each dose (200 mg) given every three weeks is $11,337, whereas the price for each dose (400 mg) given every six weeks is $22,675. Further, the drug often has different side effects rarely reported in chemotherapy treatment.

Insulin Potentiation Therapy (IPT)

Insulin Potentiation Therapy (IPT) is an alternative to chemotherapy (chemo) with fewer side effects. Sugar-hungry cancer cells are fed with insulin first to absorb chemo drug more effectively. A significantly reduced dose of chemo (e.g., 10–30 percent of the regular dose) will then be given while simultaneously strengthening the patient's immune system with IV and oral nutritional protocols. The desired outcome is more targeting while minimizing any side effects. In Arcadia Clinic in Germany, for instance, IPT is offered with "both biological anticancer agents (such as turmeric extract, resveratrol, artemisia, vitamin C, and dichloroacetic acid) and standard orthodox chemotherapy in low doses" (Saupe, 2021, p. 166). IPT is currently less widely used in the United States. Still, it is readily available in many cancer-treating clinics in Mexico or Germany.

Photodynamic Therapy

Photodynamic therapy (PDT) is a new laser therapy for treating cancer. It is a two-stage treatment combining light energy with a light-sensitive medication known as a photosensitizer to destroy cancerous and precancerous cells after the light is activated. The medication is activated by a specific wavelength of light energy from a laser, and it only becomes toxic to the targeted tumor cells after light activation. The treatment does not cause any significant side effects. Several medications are available to treat several types of cancers, such as bladder, brain, esophagus, head and neck, lung, pancreas, and skin. Previous research has shown that PDT can stimulate the immune response in the body, allowing it to destroy both cancerous and precancerous cells. In the United States, PDT is available in major cancer centers, such as the Mayo Clinic, MD Anderson Center, and Memorial Sloan Kettering Cancer Center.

Hyperthermia

Hyperthermia is a heat treatment in which body tissues are heated to an extremely high temperature, above 100 degrees Fahrenheit, to damage and kill cancer cells without harming the normal cells. During the treatment, the doctor numbs the treatment area and inserts small probes with tiny thermometers into the tumor. Hyperthermia can treat small or large body areas (local hyperthermia) or the entire body (whole-body hyperthermia). Heat is only applied to a small, affected area in local hyperthermia. In contrast, whole-body hyperthermia treats cancer that has spread throughout the body. In the latter case, the patient is placed in a thermal chamber or wrapped in hot water blankets that raise the body temperature to 108 degrees Fahrenheit for a short period. The drugs used in chemotherapy are more effective when administered along with hyperthermia, and they do not produce adverse side effects on normal cells. In addition to boosting the body's immune system, hyperthermia can improve blood circulation, which then helps in transporting the drugs into the tumor more effectively (Saupe, 2021, p. 169). Hyperthermia is not widely used to treat cancer in the United States. However, it is commonly used in clinics in Germany and Mexico.

TCM and Acupuncture

In China and increasingly in the West, acupuncture is used to alleviate the side effects of radiation and chemotherapy. Today, acupuncture has become a respectable faculty in reputable integrative medicine centers such as Duke Integrative Medicine Center, Cleveland Clinic, Memorial Sloan-Kettering Cancer Center, and MD Anderson Center. In Duke Integrative Medicine Center, for instance, acupuncture is recognized as a tool to manage pain, surgery recovery, and enhance physical therapy and rehabilitation. Acupuncture is also known to help the body improve blood and energy circulation. Major US cancer centers, such as Memorial Sloan-Kettering Cancer Center and MD Anderson Center, routinely offer acupuncture to their patients. The NIH also recognizes it as an effective chemo-related nausea and vomiting treatment. Today, acupuncture might be utilized as a supplementary therapy or a viable substitute or may be integrated into a holistic approach to managing cancer (The Moss Report, n.d.).

Aromatherapy and Essential Oils

The history of using natural essential oils derived from plants extends centuries. The history of aromatherapy is, by and large, part of the history of herbal medicine. The Arabic-speaking countries were among the first to discover the process of the distillation of oils. The knowledge then spread to the Indian subcontinent and then to Europe. The ancient practice of Ayurvedic medicine in India combines various therapeutic techniques like essential oils used in aromatherapy. The effectiveness of essential oils on cancer has been verified by many studies. Today, approximately forty different oils derived from plants are used in aromatherapy. The most popular are frankincense, lavender, peppermint, eucalyptus, chamomile, lemon, lemongrass, marjoram, geranium, rosemary, and ylang-ylang. Aromatherapy and plant-based essential oils are commonly used as complementary and alternative therapies to treat various symptoms, including cancer-related pain.

A study suggests that Ayurveda-based interventions may enhance the quality of life of cancer patients undergoing chemo-radiotherapy (Metri et al., 2013). Several studies have also been conducted on specific essential oils showing promising cancer patient benefits. For instance, a study suggests that frankincense kills cancer cells and promotes health and longevity among the neighboring non-cancerous cells, unlike chemotherapy, which targets both cancer and non-cancerous cells (Al Salmani et al., 2015). Research indicates that frankincense possesses anti-tumor properties and helps mitigate chemotherapy treatment's side effects. Lavender is also known to influence cancer prevention, and it is noted as a powerful natural antioxidant that helps reverse the damage done by free radicals. Free radical damage can lead to an array of issues like chronic illness and, more specifically, cancer. A study in Romania found that lavender possesses strong antioxidant abilities when inhaled for an hour daily (Hancianu et al., 2013).

Most patients affected by cancer develop cancer-related pain. An Italian study found significant efficacy in using essential oils to reduce the intensity of cancer-related pain (Corasaniti et al., 2023). Regarding scent, lavender was often chosen, followed by peppermint, then chamomile. Further, in a German study on using aromatherapy as an adjuvant treatment for cancer patients, some patients reported a short-term (up to two weeks posttreatment) improvement in anxiety and depression and better pain control (Boehm, Büssing, & Ostermann, 2012). Bergamot was also found to minimize the symptoms of stress-induced anxiety, mood disorders, and cancer-related pain (Bagetta et al., 2010). A Japanese study further found geranium oil to enhance tamoxifen-induced cell death (Mizuno et al., 2022). Tamoxifen is a drug prescribed by conventional doctors to prevent breast cancer.

Although the efficacy of an ancient practice of using essential oils is still being researched, the studies mentioned above have shown promising results that can help prevent and treat cancer while lessening the side effects of cancer treatment. These findings are encouraging to those looking for an alternative treatment to relieve their cancer symptoms.

Herbs, Spices, Botanicals, Vitamins, Minerals, Nutrition, Supplements

Herbal medicine is the most widespread form of medicine used in almost all parts of the world, historically and even today. The earliest herbal knowledge originates from India, spreading to China and the Middle East. Modern Western herbal medicine knowledge is borrowed from the Greeks, the philosophy of which is like Indian Ayurvedic medicine and traditional Chinese medicine, with a strong influence from the Native American tradition. Approximately 80 percent of the world's population still relies on herbal medicine for their daily health needs. Within conventional medicine, at least 20 percent of pharmaceutical drugs are derived from plants in some way.

According to a report, herbal medicine was projected to be a $129 billion market with 5.9 percent compound annual growth rate (CAGR) between 2018 and 2023 (GlobeNewswire, 2019). One of humanity's earliest anticancer remedies comes from herbs, spices, and botanicals. As discussed earlier, TCM is a vast repository of potential cancer remedies and symptoms. For instance, *artemisinin*, an extract of Chinese wormwood, was discovered by Tu Youyou, who won the Nobel Prize for her discovery in 2015. The extract is now being repurposed as a cancer remedy.

According to the Moss Report, some of the leading natural pain remedies that are supported by clinical trial data are as follows: Acupuncture, aloe vera, fish and fish oil, ginger, melatonin, mushrooms, soy, turmeric, and vitamins C, D, and E. Further, polysaccharides in vital mushrooms such as shitake and maitake activate and stimulate the body's defense and natural killer cells. When combined with enzyme preparations, these mushrooms are good supporting remedies, especially before and during chemotherapy (Saupe, 2021, p. 199).

Since 2015, approximately two dozen foods and herbs that kill cancer stem cells have been identified. Among those, the five major ones are: (1) Curcumin—from the root stem of the turmeric plant; (2) EGCG (epigallocatechin-3-gallate)—from green tea; (3) Genistein—from soybeans, soy products, and red clover; (4) Resveratrol—from skins of red grapes, plums, and berries; (5) Sulforaphane—from cruciferous vegetables such as broccoli and broccoli sprouts (Naujokat & McKee, 2020).

No wonder green tea is contained in at least 9,600 commercial products sold today! Even though one may easily find these foods, herbs, and supplements from one's local natural food stores, it still pays to consult one's healthcare provider or a certified nutritionist before embarking on any drastic diet change.

High-Dose Vitamin C and Mistletoe Injections

Some of the ingredients mentioned above can also be administered via intravenous (IV) injection to treat cancer directly. For instance, a high dose of vitamin C can be administered through an IV drip, usually in combination with other ingredients, to improve the recovery rate. Even though anyone can take vitamin C orally, the dosages are usually not high enough to significantly impact cancer cells. However, vitamin C delivered through IV bypasses the digestive tract and goes straight into the blood at a near-total absorption rate. Today, clinics in the United States have a long history of the safe use of vitamin C by IV.

Furthermore, mistletoe injection has been used mainly as an adjunct to cancer treatment in German-speaking countries such as Germany, Austria, and Switzerland. Mistletoe extracts are known to inhibit the growth of cancer cells and even kill them, mainly when applied in high doses and intravenously (Saupe, 2021, p. 199). When used alongside chemotherapy, mistletoe extracts can also reduce the side effects of chemotherapy. Today, it is easy to come across wellness clinics or "drip bars" in the United States where you can receive a hefty dose of vitamin C. However, mistletoe injections are still not as widely used in the United States. Dr. Zubin Marolia of Enlifen in India and Dr. Henning Saupe of Arcadia Clinic in Germany are among the well-known international providers who have used mistletoe injections for cancer treatment. A list of providers in complementary and alternative medicine can be found on the website of Medical Tourism Research Center (www.uncp.edu/mtrc).

Integrative Medicine

Integrative medicine combines conventional and nonconventional approaches to treatment. In other words, "complementary" medicine works with standard conventional medicine. The University of Maryland School of Medicine and the University of Arizona Andrew Weil Center for Integrative Medicine pioneered integrative medicine programs in the United States in 1994. Since then, top medical schools in the United States, such as Cleveland Clinic, Duke, Harvard Medical School, Johns Hopkins, and Mayo Clinic, have embraced the idea of integrative medicine. Each medical center is quick to rename and rebrand as a separate center in integrative medicine. Even in oncology, MD Anderson Center and Memorial Sloan-Kettering Cancer Center are among the forefronts in adopting integrative oncology.

For instance, the Duke Integrative Medicine Center's website offers customized, patient-centered health care that combines conventional medicine with proven complementary treatments. Their goal is to empower patients to embrace the healing process and lifelong wellness. Their complementary treatments include acupuncture, massage, yoga, nutrition counseling, psychotherapy, and health coaching. Its integrative treatments include physical, emotional, mental, social, spiritual, and environmental factors that affect a patient's health.

In a survey conducted among twenty-nine integrative centers in the United States, the most frequently employed practitioners were (in this order) physicians, massage therapists, meditation instructors, and acupuncturists (Horrigan et al., 2012). The same survey also asked about the use of thirty-four different interventions in treating twenty other conditions. The most frequently prescribed interventions across all conditions were (in this order) food and nutrition, supplements, yoga, meditation, TCM or acupuncture, massage, and pharmaceuticals.

Comparing two recent studies on CAM in the United States between 2012 and 2017, US adults' use of meditation and yoga has increased from 4.1 percent to 14.2 percent for meditation and 9.5 percent to 14.3 percent for yoga (Clarke et al., 2018). The corresponding increase among US children (seventeen years or younger) has also spiked from 0.6 percent to 5.4 percent for meditation and from 3.1 percent to 8.4 percent for yoga during the same period (Black et al., 2018). The slightly more significant increase in interest in yoga among children than adults within a five-year period is undoubtedly intriguing. It shows that those aged seventeen and younger increasingly embrace natural healing approaches, whether for body, mind, or spirit. Indeed, integrative medicine provides both conventional and nonconventional treatment opportunities to work together to provide patients of all ages with the best alternatives, complementing each other's needs or offsetting each other's deficiencies.

4

The Destinations: Foreign Healthcare Providers

In Chapter 2, we discussed why a potential patient from a developed nation would opt to travel for care in a developing economy, and we classified these motivations by push and pull factors. In this chapter, we will focus on some of these pull factors from the perspectives of healthcare providers in some of these destination countries. We will examine a few case studies of foreign healthcare providers in selected countries. These cases are by no means exhaustive but somewhat representative. In addition to these healthcare providers' abilities to offer significant cost savings to consumers in developed economies, most are also able to attract consumers by providing various categories for determining the quality of care, such as minimal wait time, highly personalized care, international accreditation and reputation, favorable surgical outcome, low nurse–patient ratio, good credentials of doctors, advanced medical technology and equipment, and their compliance with the HIPAA, to name a few.

On a microlevel, studies show more hospital-specific pull factors such as the availability of an in-house international patient center, the location of the hospital (e.g., distance from the airport), amenities (e.g., proximity to grocery stores, dining, and banking services), special diets offered (e.g., halal, kosher, vegetarian), and even better communication with the doctors and hospital staff are essential in the decision-making process of the medical tourists. These are opportunities and strategies that foreign healthcare providers may wish to explore to stay competitive in the globalization of the healthcare business.

Types of Hospitals

The types of foreign healthcare providers vary widely. Some are accredited by Joint Commission International (JCI). In contrast, others have various types

Table 4 Types of Foreign Healthcare Providers

Type of hospital	Examples
US-affiliated hospital	• Anadolu Medical Center in Turkey (affiliated with Johns Hopkins International) • Wockhardt Hospitals Group in India (affiliated with Harvard Medical International) • American Hospital in Dubai, UAE (affiliated with Mayo Clinic).
Private and independent hospitals—religious-based or not-for-profit	• Christus Muguerza Group in Mexico • Penang Adventist Hospital in Malaysia • St. Mary's Hospital in South Korea
Private and independent hospitals—for-profit	• Bumrungrad International Hospital in Thailand • Hospital Clinica Biblica in Costa Rica • The Specialty Hospital in Jordan
Chain of hospitals	• Acibadem Healthcare Group in Turkey • Apollo Hospitals Group in India • Raffles Medical Group in Singapore
University research or teaching hospitals	• University Hospital in Dubai (affiliated with Harvard Medical International) • National University Hospital in Singapore • Seoul National University Hospital in South Korea

Source: Compiled by author, 2023.

of ownership and affiliations with reputable US hospitals. The types of foreign healthcare providers popular among the medical tourists can be summarized in Table 4.

The hospitals listed under the chain of hospitals and University research or teaching hospitals can simultaneously be either publicly or privately owned, for-profit or not-for-profit.

Case Studies

In the following section, a few hospitals in popular medical tourism destination countries such as Turkey, Jordan, Thailand, and Singapore will be selected. Some of the pull factors that pertain to the quality of care that are considered necessary in the decision-making process of medical tourists will be highlighted. A more detailed list of these medical tourism hospitals can be found on the Medical Tourism Research Center's website at the University of North Carolina at Pembroke (uncp.edu/mtrc).

Acibadem Healthcare Group, Turkey

Turkey is strategically located between the west and the east. Acibadem (Turkish for bitter almond) healthcare group (AHG) is one of the largest private healthcare groups in Turkey, currently owning twenty-four hospitals, sixteen outpatient clinics, and other supporting service centers across four countries, that is, Turkey, Macedonia, Bulgaria, and the Netherlands. AHG employs 22,500 employees, which includes 3,500 physicians, 4,000 nurses, and the remaining support staff. The group established its very first hospital in 1991. Acibadem has its branch of urgent care, ambulance, home health, and telemedicine services known as Acibadem Mobile. Acibadem Sigorta is the insurance division that offers a diverse array of insurance services and products. Acibadem University was established in 2007 to transfer knowledge and practice from the healthcare industry to academia. It is the first university in Turkey to be set up by a healthcare group.

Strategic Location

The strategic location of Turkey between the west and the east and its easy access by air from several capital cities in Europe, the Middle East, and Central Asia has made it an attractive destination country within easy reach. Furthermore, Turkey shares cultural, historical and linguistic ties with countries in MENA (Middle East and North Africa) (e.g., Egypt, Iran, Iraq, Jordan, Lebanon, Libya, and Palestine), Central Asia (e.g., Azerbaijan, Kyrgyzstan, Uzbekistan, Kazakhstan, and Turkmenistan), and Balkan Peninsula (e.g., Albania, Bosnia and Herzegovina, Bulgaria, Kosovo, Macedonia, and Montenegro). Internally, within Turkey, one of the Acibadem hospitals in Maslak district is strategically located at one of the metro train stops that connects the commuters to Taksim Square, the central business district on the European side of Istanbul. Another branch hospital is located right next to a big shopping mall with several airport hotels nearby in the airport district known as Bakirkoy. Being strategically located near convenient infrastructure and amenities is a critical selection criterion for choosing a hospital among medical tourists.

Quality and Advanced Medical Technology

AGH received accreditation from JCI in 2005, 2008, 2010, and 2011. Acibadem group is known for its advanced medical equipment for cancer and neurosurgery, including Cyberknife, trilogy, 3 Tesla MRI, Gamma knife, and a large number of DaVinci robots in Turkey.

Acibadem Technology, as part of the group, began operating in 2015. It has developed products such as "Cerebral Plus" to manage the hospital information system and allow quick access to hospital records with the capability of using foreign languages. The software was so successful and popular that the group could generate revenues by selling it to other healthcare providers domestically and internationally (Üner et al., 2021). Acibadem Technology also develops other products such as "Astore," which is a medication management system, "Lab Assistant" (lab information system), and "Acibadem" Online (a patient portal) (Acibadem Technology, 2023). They publish their general outcome data, such as in-patient mortality rates and surgical infection rates, in their in-house literature but not on their websites (Ataoglu, 2012).

Integrated Billing

Like most international hospitals, Acibadem hospitals offer medical tourists integrated billing, that is, charges for physician and hospital services, laboratory tests, and pharmacy prescriptions, which are included in a single bill (Ataoglu, 2012). International patients can get free quotes by filling out an online query form on the hospital websites. For international patients with insurance coverage or those sponsored by their governments, the Acibadem hospital group works with their insurance companies or embassies by sending the medical bills directly to them. However, patients must pay the entire amount before treatments for services not covered by third-party payers.

International Patients and Their Service Center

Turkey received 1.25 million medical tourists in 2022, generating more than $2 billion in health tourism revenue (Loss, 2023). Medical tourists in Turkey spend an average of $1,103 per person, twice that of tourists who come for other purposes. AHG serves approximately 3.5 million patients nationally and worldwide annually, including half a million international patients from more than 100 nations (Üner et al., 2021). According to one hospital source, the composition of the medical tourists relative to the total number of patients is approximately 6 percent per year, with a projected growth of 10 percent yearly. The most sought-after treatments by international patients are oncology, cardiology, neural surgeries, and pediatric surgeries. The top three groups of international patients come from neighboring Iraq, Iran, Syria, and Libya, followed by Russia and those in the Balkan Peninsula (Ataoglu, 2012). While the Russians tend to seek oncology and bone marrow transplants, patients from the

Balkans are inclined to seek kidney and liver transplants in addition to cancer treatment.

Another selection criterion for hospital choice for medical tourists is whether an in-house international patient center (IPC) is available. Acibadem group boasts an IPC that hires at least 100 staff. The primary functions of the center are extensive, including online medical consultation and cost estimation, appointment scheduling, assistance in hospital admission and discharge, international medical insurance, post-care, language interpretation, local sightseeing, and arrangements for accommodation and transportation. The staff provides at least twenty language interpretations that include Bosnian, Bulgarian, English, German, Macedonian, Romanian, Russian, and Serbian (Ataoglu, 2012). The hospital websites can be viewed in sixteen other languages besides Turkish. One of the value-added services provided by the IPC is the accompaniment of patients to their appointments and the translation of treatment-related educational materials for non-Turkish-speaking patients at no additional costs (Ataoglu, 2012).

Strategic Partnership

AHG partnered with Harvard Medical International in 2003 to promote the high level of professional development of medical professionals in the network (Woodman, 2008). The group also cooperates with Massachusetts General Hospital to develop software for advanced MRI technology. Acibadem is currently the only Turkish hospital that engages in an international expansion through a management contract to provide managerial and operation know-how to a hospital in Iraq (Üner et al., 2021). The group also forms a strategic alliance with the Iraqi government, resulting in the latter sending a chartered flight with thirty to seventy patients for treatments from time to time at Acibadem hospitals (Ataoglu, 2012). The group also has contracted directly with American corporate employers such as General Electric and Unilever and American insurance companies such as Aetna, Cigna, and Allianz. The contracted or referred patients may receive a 15–20 percent treatment discount in such cases (Ataoglu, 2012).

Similarly, international or domestic medical tourism agents may initiate a similar partnership with Acibadem by referring private patients to their hospitals, often earning a percentage-based commission fee in return (Ataoglu, 2012). Furthermore, the group has established affiliations with Macedonia, Albania, and Serbia hospitals. The partnership often includes patient referrals, especially those of complex diagnostics and procedures, sharing expertise, consultation services, staff training, and education.

So why Turkey? A potential medical tourist, at some point, will ask this question. For history buffs, there are miles of Byzantium wall and ruins to explore around the Istanbul areas, and other exciting sites include Hagia Sophia with its rare Christian mosaics, Sultanahmet mosque, the maiden tower, the famous bazaar, all featured in earlier James Bond movies. On the Asian side of Turkey, there are many cities and towns such as Ephesus, Izmir (ancient Smyrna), and Antakya (or Antioch), where the Apostle Paul had set foot around the first century during four of his well-known missionary journeys.

Two Hospitals in Jordan

Jordan has emerged as a preferred medical tourism destination country, especially in the Middle East and North Africa (MENA) market. Jordan is well known for its high-quality medical services, with highly qualified doctors, nurses, pharmacists, and medical engineers. The first open heart surgery performed in Jordan was in 1970. Subsequently, the first kidney transplant was performed in 1972, and the first heart transplant was performed in 1985.

Jordan currently has 121 hospitals; among them are ten hospitals accredited by JCI (The Private Hospitals Association, n.d.). Jordan has more than 35,000 physicians, with around 60 percent working in the private sector. Most physicians are board-certified in the United States, the UK, Europe, and Canada. The hospitals in Jordan invest heavily in the latest medical technology, such as MRI, CT scan, nuclear imaging, and IVF equipment, which are standard in most private hospitals in Jordan. The Jordanian government has implemented an e-health system to set up health records that are easy to access among all public and university hospitals.

Approximately a quarter of a million international patients travel to Jordan annually for treatment, bringing a revenue of over US$1 billion (The Private Hospitals Association, n.d.). These patients originate mainly from the MENA. Popular treatments medical tourists in Jordan seek are general surgery, heart surgery, neurosurgery, oncology, orthopedics, pediatrics, and IVF.

Jordan Hospital, Jordan

Jordan Hospital (JH) is a private hospital with 300 beds. It was opened in 1996 and is accredited by theJCI and the International Society for Quality (ISQua) in health care. Most doctors in JH are trained in the United States, the UK, Europe, and Canada. JH provides specialized therapeutic units for emergency medicine, imaging and interventional radiology, nuclear medicine, and renal analysis. It offers specialty clinics for diabetes, endocrinology, osteoporosis, IVF, men's disease, and obesity. JH is also recognized for its postgraduate training in surgery, medicine, obstetrics, and gynecology by the Jordanian Medical Council. Its medical department provides training programs for consultants from the Gulf Cooperation Council (GCC) countries and college students from Jordan and the Arab world. GCC comprises Saudi Arabia, Bahrain, Oman, Qatar, Kuwait, and the United Arab Emirates (UAE).

Medical tourism is one of JH's primary sources of revenue. It served more than 7,000 international patients in 2007 (Woodman, 2008). In 2021, Yemen was ranked top regarding international patients received in JH (Khartan, 2021). Other countries from which international patients originate are Palestine, Iraq, Syria, and GCC countries. The United States was rated ten in terms of the volume of international patients received in JH. International patients typically come to JH for general surgery, cardiac surgery, neurosurgery, orthopedics, fertility, and IVF treatments. JH is incredibly proud of its organ transplantation programs, which include bone marrow, cornea, kidney, and liver. Notably, JH maintains its apartments on hospital property to serve its recovering patients, including its international patients.

Specialty Hospital, Jordan

The Specialty Hospital (SH) is another private hospital in Jordan with 265 beds. It has been open since 1993 and is one of the oldest hospitals in Jordan. It is a general hospital with all the medical services a patient may expect. It also has a dedicated medical tourism department designated for all international patients. In 2017, the SH was ranked as one of the top ten medical tourism destination hospitals worldwide by the Medical Travel Quality Alliance (MTQUA) (Manneh, 2021). In 2018 and 2019, SH was ranked the third-best hospital in medical tourism worldwide by the MTQUA. The hospital has been JCI-accredited since 2008 and has earned accreditation for five cycles. In 2017 (renewed again in 2020), they received two JCI disease-specific certifications, one in acute myocardial infarction and another in heart failure program (Manneh, 2021). SH is the only one in Jordan and the seventh in the world to earn two JCI disease-specific certifications. Further, the US White House Medical Unit visited the SH in 2018. They selected and visited SH to make plans in case of a medical emergency, presumably during a potential US presidential visit.

International Patients

Until 2019, Saudi Arabia was ranked top among the medical tourists visiting SH. In 2021, Iraq was ranked a top country where medical tourists originate. Patients from neighboring GCC and African countries (Chad, Sudan) also travel to Jordan for medical care. They come for major surgeries such as cardiac diseases, neurosurgery, advanced surgeries such as transcatheter aortic valve implantation (TAVI), heart surgery, leadless pacemakers, and orthopedics like knee replacement (Manneh, 2021). Many also come for kidney transplants, being accompanied by a first-degree donor, as required by Jordanian law. The SH is ranked number one in kidney transplants in terms of the number of transplants and success rate. They also perform many cases of bone marrow transplants for pediatrics and adults, as well as in oncology and IVF with gender selection. They also receive a fair number of Jordanians who work abroad and are returning home for medical care.

Selection Criteria

Factors that attract medical tourists to Jordan, particularly the SH, are low wait time, quality of care, international accreditations, and affordability. Some treatments can be performed on the same day as the appointment. SH takes pride in its two MRIs, two CT scans, abundant X-rays and ultrasounds, three cath labs, twenty-one operating theaters (Manneh, 2021), staff who speak Arabic and English, and similar culture and religion in the region. All medical records are available in English; however, they receive fewer English-speaking patients than they would like. Regarding the strategic alliance, SH has agreements with big corporations that provide direct insurance to their employees and contracts with international insurance companies, foreign medical tourism facilitators, and other foreign hospitals. Interestingly, as in the case of South Korea, it is considered illegal for Jordanian medical tourism facilitators to operate their business domestically in Jordan. For that reason, SH works with foreign medical tourism facilitators from countries such as Algeria, Kurdistan, Sudan, and Chad to bring in volumes of patients.

Why should one consider Jordan? Jordan boasts its Rose Red city of Petra, one of the world's seven wonders. Ma'in Hot Springs and the Dead Sea, the earth's lowest point, attract tourists to their natural health and spa resorts.

Bumrungrad International Hospital, Thailand

At the peak of the growth of medical tourism, the number of international patients received by Thailand grew at an average of 10 percent annually, reaching

1 million in 2005, compared to 500,000 in India and 250,000 in Singapore during the same period. Approximately 55,000 Americans were treated there during the same year, 30 percent more than the previous year (Kher, 2006). About 83 percent of them had non-cosmetic procedures. The success of Thailand as a medical tourism destination has been attributed to high medical quality in areas such as cosmetic surgery, cardiac operation, hip and knee resurfacing, a large pool of Western-trained medical specialists, and the hospitality and friendliness of the Thai people.

Bumrungrad, the largest private hospital in Southeast Asia, is currently an undisputable leader of medical tourism in the region. Currently listed on the Thai stock exchange, Bumrungrad was among the first hospitals in Asia to receive its JCI accreditation in 2002, followed by at least seventeen more Thai facilities that have received the international healthcare quality endorsement since then. Bumrungrad boosts its upscale facilities: a lobby with marble floors, expensive and comfortable chairs, and valet parking. It also owns twenty-one VIP suites, which can be easily mistaken as a five-star hotel or a shopping mall. McDonald's and Japanese and Italian restaurants are on the mezzanine floor above Starbucks. As one description goes, "The hospital interior is furnished and decorated to create a rather lavish and comfortable, but modern ambiance. Non-medical staffers wear traditional Thai silk servant dresses instead of respect-demanding white coats" (Veerasoontorn, Beise-Zee, and Sivayathorn, 2011). Bumrungrad Hospital benefitted indirectly from the aftermath of 9/11, as patients from the Middle East began to take a shorter flight to Southeast Asian countries such as Thailand, Malaysia, and Singapore instead of Europe and North America to avoid discrimination and visa problems.

Doctors' Credentials

Out of approximately 1,400 doctors affiliated with Bumrungrad, about 300, or 21 percent, have US board certification (Knowledge at Wharton Podcast, 2009). About 25 percent of the doctors are full-time staff. The remaining are part-time staff teaching at the university and working at the hospital in the evenings and on weekends. Some of the doctors have European and Australian training experience.

Integrated Information System and Advanced Medical Technology

As early as 2007, Bumrungrad had entirely digitized the patient paper records into a single integrated database. The database includes registration, admission, appointments, medical records, laboratory results, pharmacy, and finance information. The new information system allows medical personnel to access patients' immediate records anywhere in the hospital, thus effectively improving patient and doctor communication. Furthermore, Bumrungrad is continuing to upgrade its medical technology to ensure that patients perceive the high quality of diagnosis and treatment. Advanced medical equipment, such as MRI, 64-slice CT scanner, and image-guided radiotherapy (IGRT), has been adopted relatively early. As early as 2010, the hospital had already implemented a "pharmacy robot," a fully automated drug management system to replace routine human tasks and improve patient care and safety (Veerasoontorn, Beise-Zee, and Sivayathorn, 2011).

International Patients and International Medical Coordination Office (IMCO)

In 2019, Bumrungrad International Hospital in Bangkok had over 1.1 million patients, 665,000 (or 60 percent) of those patients being international patients, so on average, 11,000 patients per week, as compared to Cleveland Clinic in Ohio with 11,000 international patients a year in 2019 (Boucher, 2021). As early as 2009, international patients from approximately 190 countries had already made up approximately 42 percent of the total patient volumes in Bumrungrad and approximately 55 percent of their revenues (Knowledge at Wharton Podcast, 2009). This was due mainly to higher-end procedures sought by international patients. The hospital's regional patients come from Vietnam, Cambodia, Burma, and Bangladesh. Middle Eastern patients' volume increased from 12,000 in 2001 by tenfold during the decade following 9/11. The American patients tend to come to Bumrungrad for cost, saving them 50–80 percent on joint or heart operations for uninsured or underinsured. The European patients tend to come for a shorter waitlist on their operations, being on most social insurance programs. Middle Eastern patients tend to come for the perceived higher quality of medical expertise and a much better quality of care. About 40 percent of international patients are repeat patients or have heard about the hospital through friends or family (Knowledge at Wharton Podcast, 2009).

Bumrungrad has representative offices in at least twenty-two countries. Potential patients can contact people who speak their language in these offices and coordinate their trips. Once they arrive in Thailand, the International Medical Coordination Office (IMCO) has interpreters who can speak up to 110 languages that can further coordinate their needs. The IMCO comprises twenty-five doctors and nurses who can schedule appointments, make local arrangements, and coordinate pre- and post-care. The office also has a travel and visa section that assists patients in extending their visas at the embassies or taking in some local sightseeing. It also offers a meet-and-greet service at the airport. In addition, as in Jordan Hospital, Bumrungrad has two adjoining hotels on the hospital property, one a three-star and another a four-star, to accommodate patients and their loved ones.

Thailand has become a popular destination for medical tourists due to its affordable hospitals, the quality of the staff, and state-of-the-art medical technologies. It is also widely famous among Americans as a holiday destination. Phuket Island, Koh Samui, picturesque Phang Nga Bay, and James Bond Island are among the popular beach resorts frequented by American tourists.

Raffles Medical Group, Singapore

Raffles Medical Group was founded in 1976 with two clinics and received its JCI accreditation in 2008. The group is currently listed on the mainboard of the Singapore Stock Exchange, and it operates in fourteen cities in five Asian countries (China, Hong Kong, Japan, Vietnam, and Cambodia). The group includes three tertiary hospitals with over 100 multidisciplinary clinics, bringing in a revenue of $707 million in 2023, an increase of 24 percent over the previous year (Raffles Medical Group, 2023). The main center of the integrated private tertiary hospital is strategically located in the heart of the city of Singapore, conveniently close to the restaurants and shopping centers. It operates over thirty-one specialist centers and specialist satellite clinics, covering at least thirty disciplines. Disciplines covered include orthopedics, cardiology, oncology, obstetrics and gynecology, and dental services. The main hospital also offered integrative medicine, such as traditional Chinese medicine (TCM), since 2005. Services included are TCM herbs, *TuiNa* massage, in addition to acupuncture. Raffles Hospital also manages a 24/7 airport clinic at Singapore's Changi International Airport and Hong Kong International Airport, catering to the needs of travelers and transit passengers. Today, the group has around 3,000 employees, including 430 physicians, serving approximately 2.8 million patients and 7,000 corporate clients annually (Raffles Medical Group, 2023). Even though the hospital has a twenty-four-hour emergency center, its air ambulance service is outsourced to a third party. Raffles Health Insurance is the insurance arm of the group, and it partners with *Bupa Global* (bupaglobal.com), a British-based insurance group, to provide insurance needs to individuals and international corporate clients.

Quality of Care

Raffles Hospital has received Singapore Quality Class certification and ISO 9000 certification, which attest to the hospital's quality improvement system. *Raffles Connect* is an app that allows patients to make appointments, stay current with their medical records, order health supplements, and even consult a doctor via video.

According to a hospital source, Raffles Hospital differentiates itself from other hospitals in Singapore by its adoption of the Group Practice Model (GPM) and team-based care across departments (Soo, 2012). Under GPM, all physicians at Raffles are full-time staff focused on serving patients within their specialized disciplines while their supporting staff take care of administration and logistics. Under such a model, specialists work as a team to provide quality assurance of medical services that are integrated, peer-reviewed, and medically accredited. The team-based care benefits patients with multiple conditions who require more than one doctor. Patients are diagnosed and treated quickly and efficiently. As doctors conform to the group's fee schedules, no unnecessary repeat consultations or examinations are performed, thus keeping the patient's medical bill low. For post-care communications with offshore doctors of international patients, physicians from Raffles usually communicate with them through email or teleconferencing (Soo, 2012).

International Patients and International Patient Center (IPC)

The international patients constitute 30 percent of Raffles' total patients. The top three nationalities of their international patients are from Indonesia, Russia, Myanmar, and Vietnam (Soo, 2012). The top five treatments international patients seek are orthopedic surgery (knee and joint replacements), heart surgery (stent), oncology, general surgery, and health screening. Like other top medical tourism hospitals, Raffles has its in-house international patient department, consisting of a twenty-staff marketing department that provides concierge services such as arranging care and accommodations for patients and language translation services. The center has an impressive and comfortable lounge equipped with two personal desktop computers connected to the Internet, tea or coffee snack facilities, and a small library. International patients or their companions were seen using the PCs or chatting with their doctors in the relaxing lounge. According to a hospital source, 35–40 percent of the international patients enquired about local sightseeing tours from the IPC while in Singapore (Soo, 2012), indicating that they potentially engaged in tourism and contributed towards the tourism revenues of the Singapore economy.

Marketing and Strategic Partnerships

According to one hospital source, many international patients heard about Raffles Hospital through word of mouth instead of print media such as magazines or, lately, the Internet (Soo, 2012). Raffles Hospital practiced selective advertising and targeted marketing. The staff sometimes travels to client countries to talk publicly and establish contacts with local doctors. Furthermore, Raffles Hospital operates a network of international referral agencies outside Singapore. These are foreign travel agencies or foreign medical tourism facilitators that can direct international patients to Raffles Hospital. These international referral agencies are primarily in neighboring Southeast Asian countries, such as Indonesia, Malaysia, Vietnam, Cambodia, and Bangladesh. The foreign facilitators usually take the initiative to contact the hospital; Raffles usually separates the physician fees and then offers percentage commissions based on the facilities that are being utilized.

Pricing and Insurance

Treatment fee structures of Raffles Hospital are generally fixed, and they are published on their website as well as in printed brochures. Raffles Hospital does not practice a two-tier pricing system; that is, both domestic and international patients are charged the same rate (Soo, 2012). The first-time physician consultation fee is $125, followed by approximately $90 for each subsequent visit within a year. Raffles Hospital practices integrated billing. Patients can request bills from various specialties or departments (e.g., dental clinic and TCM department) to be integrated into one single bill as long as the treatments are received within the same day (Soo, 2012).

Moreover, Raffles Hospital has consolidated and direct billing arrangements with many US and European insurance companies such as Aetna, Cigna, Blue Cross Blue Shield, Bupa, Europ Assistance, and Mondial Assistance (Soo, 2012). These arrangements are usually the results of a both-way initiation process; often, the hospital learns about a foreign insurance company through their international patients. In addition, the hospital's corporate department works with multinational corporations (MNCs) to offer corporate rates for a comprehensive range of medical, dental, and TCM services and physical examinations for their employees.

Legal Recourse and HIPAA

Physicians in Raffles Hospital are classified as (1) full-time doctors, (2) sessional-contract doctors, and (3) visiting doctors (visit the hospital two–three times per week). Raffles has its malpractice clauses known as the Medical Protection Society (MPS). Under the Singapore MPS, the annual premium for internal medicine is around US$1,200 per year. Singapore passed a HIPAA equivalent law called the *Personal Data Protection Act* in 2014, updated in 2023. In the hospital brochure entitled "Patient Charter," it is stated that "patients be accorded privacy while in the facility and confidentiality of all information and records regarding their care" under the section on "Patients' Rights and Responsibilities." Such a charter is merely a commonsense guideline put out by the hospital. In addition, international patients are usually required to sign consent forms for treatment and biopsy.

Singapore is selected as a destination country for medical tourists mainly because it is a modern city nation in which English is widely spoken. Some well-known tourist attractions are Marina Bay Promenade, the Botanic Garden, Sentosa Island, Chinatown, and the diverse cultural heritage and cuisine.

Now that you've checked out a sample of the selected international healthcare providers and what they offer to medical tourists, your next move is to figure out which one best suit your needs, get in touch with them, and find out how to get there. A list of current healthcare providers and facilitators can be found on the website of Medical Tourism Research Center (www.uncp.edu/mtrc). That brings us to the medical tourism facilitators, which is what the next chapter is about.

5

The Middlemen: Medical Tourism Facilitators

As mentioned in Chapter 1, the medical tourism market is a fast-growing and lucrative industry with an expected growth of 13 percent to 15 percent between 2019 and 2027, expected to reach a potential value of $275 billion by 2027. Given that the facilitator industry is mainly self-regulated, with such potential growth and profits from the medical tourism market, it is a small wonder that as many as 150 such firms have sprung up across the United States since 2007. Due to asymmetric information and high search costs, as pointed out in Chapter 1, an average medical tourist in America is likely to know very little about destination countries, foreign healthcare providers, and the services they have to offer. Therefore, they may engage in services the intermediary or the medical tourism facilitator provides. Most medical tourists find out about the services of these facilitators through an Internet search. However, a small percentage may find out through word of mouth from friends and family. The author has combed through scores of these websites from previous research; unfortunately, there is very little evidence of pricing transparency on facilitators' websites and very little information about even the history of when each company was set up. Thus, it is challenging for medical tourists to select a particular facilitator. As such, many potential medical tourists search for more than one company to compare prices and services. Unfortunately, as in health care and travel, facilitator services are like "experienced" goods or services; you must experience the service firsthand before knowing the quality. Knowing what to look for when selecting a facilitator will help a potential medical tourist minimize such an experience.

In this chapter, we will discuss the market structure of the facilitators' industry, the assorted services they provide, how they operate and compete in this business, how they differentiate and advertise themselves to potential medical tourists, and eventually, the future of this market.

Market Structure

The market for medical tourism facilitators or medical tourism concierge services bears a resemblance to *monopolistic competition*. It has the market characteristics that are featured in Table 5. Each firm occupies a small percentage of the total market share. There are low barriers to entry into the market, as the start-up cost is low, such as a PC with a website setup, some knowledge of foreign hospitals, and essential travel information. The cost of operation grows with the customer base. The easy entry and exit from the facilitator market and the large number of sellers in the industry explain the high turnover rate among these firms. Although several firms in operation in 2013 had provided facilitator services since 2004, many left the industry after only two years or less (Gan & Frederick, 2015).

Given that becoming a facilitator can be as simple as posting relevant health and hospital information on a website, it is not surprising that there is a broad spectrum of types of facilitators. There are diverse motivations for starting the facilitator's business. For instance, numerous firms were formed after their owners needed medical attention while traveling abroad. Many facilitators are merely extensions of travel agencies. Some were founded by physicians or those in the United States who had family ties to the destination countries. The size of the facilitators varies as well. It ranges from a large corporate office offering many choices of hospitals in several countries to a modest office providing fewer hospitals in a single country. As odd as it may sound, many operate out of homes without a physical office.

Due to *economies of scope*, many facilitators were created by people with prior experience in the tourism industry. In one study, 9 percent of the 173 websites

Table 5 Market Characteristics of Facilitators Industry

Market Characteristics	
Many firms	√
Each firm has a small market share	√
Low barrier to entry and exit	√
Imperfect information of consumer	√
Independent price setting	√
Product and service differentiation	√
Advertising	√

surveyed retained connections with travel agencies (Gan & Frederick, 2011). Sharing common skills with a travel agency should be helpful to a facilitator. Travel agencies' knowledge of conducting business in foreign countries, for instance, arranging flights and accommodations and assisting with visas, would apply to the medical tourism business. Further, suppose a facilitator has a connection with a travel agency. In that case, the former should be able to book travel arrangements directly through the latter, omitting the need to deal with a third-party firm. Using such affiliates should improve the facilitator's ability to provide value-added service to potential medical tourists.

In this market, where facilitators know more about foreign healthcare providers than potential consumers, they compete by differentiating their services mainly through web advertising. They do so by offering various pricing structures, providing value-added services, and demonstrating various quality indicators on their websites.

Pricing Schemes

The facilitators set their prices independently of others, offering various pricing schemes (see Table 6). While some services are bundled as a package by some agents at a fixed price, others are offered individually and are charged separately. The "all-inclusive" package price typically includes treatment, round-trip airfares, and hotel expenses. The treatment costs cover hospitalization, physician fees, nursing care, medications, and external therapies. Some facilitators may charge a concierge fee of $200–$500 for their referrals and the standard treatment costs. However, others may charge a percentage-based commission for all the services

Table 6 Pricing Structures of Facilitators

Pricing Scheme	Explanation
Concierge fee	A flat fee that excludes treatment and travel costs.
Concierge fee plus treatment cost	Excludes travel costs.
All-inclusive pricing	Includes treatment and travel costs.
Commission-based fee	A fee as a percentage of all treatment and travel costs the facilitator arranges.
Free of charge	The facilitator will receive a referral fee from the foreign healthcare providers.

they help arrange. Some agents advertise free service. In such cases, they receive a direct referral fee from foreign healthcare providers. Potential patients will do themselves a favor by finding out what a "package" would entail at the beginning stage of their inquiries and before they commit to any payment.

In order to avoid *free-riding* problems, the facilitators usually know how to arbitrate between providing too much information before receiving payments and providing too little information and losing a customer. Suppose the facilitator provides too much information at the beginning. In that case, there is a risk of losing a potential patient to a direct channel, such as a foreign hospital. On the other hand, if too little information is provided, the potential patients may switch to a different facilitator, or they may decide not to seek offshore treatment after all. According to a brief survey conducted by a facilitator, out of the 150 patients surveyed, 67 percent of them contacted more than one agent. Of course, one way to solve the free-riding problem is for the facilitator to collect payment at the appropriate level of the potential patient's decision process. Most facilitators only charge when the travel arrangements are made. Such practice reflects the agents' awareness of the alternative services available to medical tourists.

Service Scope

The main job of a facilitator is to connect a potential patient to a foreign healthcare provider. However, there is much variation in the facilitators' scope of services. On one end of the spectrum, some facilitators only provide information about foreign hospitals and arrange air transportation, relying on the hospitals to provide most services. On the other end of the spectrum, better-established facilitators would arrange visa application and pre-care, have medical records transmitted and translated, arrange for a companion or a nurse to accompany the patient, find suitable accommodations during convalescence, arrange for post-care, and coordinate communication between foreign health care providers and the US doctors.

These extra services, or ancillary services, are another way the facilitators differentiate themselves from each other. These ancillary services can also include the assistance of a case manager, the provision of optional tour and spa packages, and the option to select from various insurance.

Many facilitators often use case managers stationed in the United States. A basic level of case management involves a representative in the destination country who will handle ground transportation, such as airport pickup and drop-off. In more advanced case management, the case managers may even accompany the patient to doctor's appointments and stay with the patient on the day of surgery or the day after surgery, though at additional cost.

The facilitators may also coordinate various degrees of pre- and post-care medical support services. They usually include facilitating communications between the patient's home physician and the foreign doctor, scheduling appointments with doctors in their home country for pre-trip diagnostic tests and post-trip follow-up checks, and transcribing and sending medical records. Some facilitators also provide medical escort services, such as nurses who accompany patients from their home countries to foreign hospitals, or they may use an air ambulance service. Personal care nurses can also be hired through supporting firms such as Homewatch CareGivers (homewatchcaregivers.com) to accompany the patient during recuperation in a foreign hotel.

The facilitators also vary in the kinds of optional services they promote on their websites—some offer to arrange vacation packages and spa services for patients while they are in destination countries. Spa services promote healthy lifestyles, well-being, and stress relief. They can include acupuncture, aromatherapy, herbal healing, homeopathy, massage, and yoga.

Many facilitators offer travel insurance covering costs incurred when a trip gets canceled or a medical emergency arises. Insurance against medical complications is not as standard, but a few facilitators offer it. For instance, Surgery Planet (surgeryplanet.com), based in Concord, California, offers medical complications or "travel medical" insurance through Seven Corners. Medical Tourism Corporation (medicaltourismco.com) also offers similar "medical tourism" insurance. Such insurance can also be obtained independently from Global Protective Solutions (globalprotectivesolutions.com), Global Healthcare Connections, Inc. (globalhealthcareconnections.com), and WeExpats Insurance Solutions (weexpats.com). The medical complications policy would pay for such things as surgery needed and related expenses to correct problems that arise during the surgery abroad and the costs of rescheduling flights because of an unexpectedly long recovery period. Some facilitators may arrange financing through third parties. Financing options can include medical loans or even flexible payment options linked to retirement.

Service Differentiation

In addition to service scope, which can be a differentiating strategy, the facilitators also differentiate how they refer their potential patients to foreign healthcare providers. Some only connect with foreign healthcare providers in a single country. In contrast, others offer various countries and hospitals to refer potential patients. The Internet is one of the key factors fueling the growth of medical tourism, as it allows consumers easy access to information and provides the facilitators the means to advertise their services. In the following section, we will examine how facilitators differentiate themselves from others by examining three different aspects of information they advertise on their websites.

Information on Destination Countries

The primary function of facilitators is to refer potential consumers to foreign healthcare providers in destination countries. On the part of facilitators, this will involve networking or partnering with healthcare providers in destination countries and gaining basic travel information about these countries. For instance, facilitators may want to research the visa requirements, hotel accommodation, exchange rates, weather, and customs of a destination country and then provide the info to their consumers. Some agents work with only one foreign hospital in a single country or a small number of foreign hospitals in a single country. For instance, IndUShealth, based in Raleigh, North Carolina, only refers potential patients to healthcare providers in India. European Medical Tourist (europeanmedicaltourist.com), based in Austin, Texas, only refers to clinics in Germany. Nevertheless, other facilitators work with many foreign hospitals in many countries. For instance, Placid Way (placidway.com), based in Denver, Colorado, works with hospitals in over fifty countries.

A review of facilitators' websites by Gan and Frederick (2011) shows that the five most popular country destinations referred by the facilitators are India, Singapore, Thailand, Costa Rica, and Mexico. Other emerging countries popular with US medical tourists are Malaysia, the Philippines, South Korea, and Taiwan in Asia; Argentina, Brazil, Columbia, El Salvador, and Guatemala among Latin American countries; Jordan, Turkey, United Arab Emirates, and South Africa in the Middle East and Africa (MENA) region.

Information on Destination Hospitals

Just as some facilitators differentiate themselves in the number of countries they refer their potential consumers, some agents specialize in only one or two hospitals, while some claim to send patients to hundreds of hospitals. Instead of merely stating the number of hospitals used, it is essential for the facilitators to explicitly name the hospitals they refer their consumers to on their websites. In selecting a particular hospital, in addition to international accreditation and reputation, more experienced consumers may also look for the following hospital-related variables advertised on the facilitator's website:

- quality of care (e.g., process and surgical outcomes, nurse–patient ratio),
- credentials and training of foreign physicians (e.g., if they speak English and if they have any specialty training in the United States),
- advanced medical technology and equipment
- HIPAA compliance.

Even if the hospitals are identified, detailed information may not be readily available on the facilitators' websites. Facilitators who visited the destination hospitals and conducted their own research are more likely to add value to consumers because they have firsthand knowledge.

Information on Types of Treatment

One can expect the facilitators to differ in the nature and amount of information they provide consumers on their websites. Studies have shown that consumers are most interested in the quality of the information on a health-related website. Consumers desire a breadth and depth of information. However, more importantly, they want to be able to find information about the specific medical problem that concerns them. Some facilitator's sites provide great educational information, including detailed diagrams of treatment procedures popularly sought by medical tourists. Such information is usually provided through links to websites such as WebMD or the National Institute of Health's MedLine Plus.

The types of procedure normally advertised on facilitators' websites can be grouped under the following broad categories:

- medical (e.g., coronary artery bypass graft (CABG), knee or hip replacement),
- weight-loss procedures (e.g., gastric bypass, lap band),
- cosmetic or plastic surgery (e.g., facelift, breast augmentation),
- dental (e.g., crowns, implants, and root canals),
- vision (e.g., LASIK).

The respective procedures popularly sought by medical tourists among the popular country destinations are as follows: India is known for its orthopedic surgery, especially in knee resurfacing and cardiac care; Singapore for its cancer treatment, spinal surgery, and transplants; Thailand for its orthopedic, cosmetic, and cardiac procedures. Due to its proximity to the United States, Mexico is conveniently located and well known for its dental work, and Costa Rica for its orthopedic, spinal, liposuction, and other cosmetic procedures (Rosenthal, 2009).

Quality Indicators of Facilitators

Some facilitators demonstrate a few quality indicators to assure consumers of the quality of their services and, ultimately, to differentiate themselves from other firms. These quality indicators are mainly their strategic partnership with other players in the market, their exclusive dealings with hospitals with good credentials, the relevant industry experience of their staff, and the stamp of approval from third-party endorsement bodies such as the Better Business Bureau.

Partnerships with Other Players

It is common for facilitators to form partnerships with key industry players to create a start-to-finish experience for potential patients and allow value to be built at each step along a patient's medical journey. Many facilitators partner strategically with third-party payers such as corporate employers or insurance companies. Examples of such partnerships were the relationship between WorldMed Assist and Swiss Re and the agreement between Companion Global Healthcare and BasicPlus Health Insurance in the 2000s. Unfortunately, both facilitators mentioned are no longer in the medical tourism business today. Such a partnership can be mutually beneficial. The facilitator can increase its leverage by gaining access to the pool of potential patients provided by the insurance companies or employers. The facilitator also gains an implicit stamp of approval from the third-party payers, which can signal quality for a facilitator. Potential patients will consider this a key differentiating element when choosing an intermediary.

With the evolvement of the medical tourism industry, facilitators are increasingly supported by firms with complementary and niche services. Examples are independent air ambulances and those specializing in home care, such as Homewatch CareGivers. Moreover, major international airlines and hotel chains are developing innovative services that complement the medical tourism market. A good example is Thai Airways and Air India, which award frequent flyer mileage to medical travelers flying to Thailand or India. Lufthansa Airlines uniquely offers air ambulance service on their scheduled commercial flights. Further, Continental International coordinates with hospitals to accommodate patients during their recuperations; Village Hotel and Residences across from Raffles Hospitals in Singapore offer a discount package for medical tourists and their companions. Partnering with some support firms and hospitality-related industries will help facilitators differentiate themselves, giving them a competitive advantage.

Good Hospital Credentials

Foreign healthcare providers are the final destinations for medical tourists on their medical journey. These healthcare providers typically demonstrate their quality by having Western-trained doctors, international accreditations from the Joint Commission International (JCI) or the International Organization for Standardization (ISO), or affiliations with reputable US hospitals. JCI is an arm of the body that accredits most US hospitals to improve quality of care and safety. US-affiliated hospitals would make Americans feel more comfortable, especially if post-care services are needed upon returning home. Some higher-end facilitators refer their potential consumers exclusively to JCI-accredited, ISO-certified, or US-affiliated hospitals to differentiate themselves.

In addition to the JCI accreditation standards, notable accreditation standards exist outside the United States, such as the International Society for Quality and Safety in Healthcare (IsQua), QHA Trent Accreditation (UK), Accreditation Canada International (ACI), and Australian Council on Healthcare Standards (ACSH). Some of these standards are displayed on the websites of medical tourism facilitators outside the United States.

Dealing exclusively with JCI-accredited, ISO-certified, or US-affiliated hospitals may indicate better quality of the facilitators' services. The exclusive dealing will differentiate them from others, allowing them to outperform their competitors.

Relevant Industry Experience

Some facilitators have prior experience in relevant industries, such as travel agencies, insurance companies, or healthcare professionals. Physicians founded some firms, and others have physicians in their top management. There are things a physician would be more likely to stress than facilitator executives who do not have medical experience. For instance, it is crucial to use JCI-accredited hospitals and coordinate post-care with the patient's US physician. Further, having medical professionals should increase the firm's credibility in providing proper diligence in its evaluations of doctors and hospitals. Having a physician as a founder or on the top-level management team can be considered a quality indicator. After the potential patients make their first contact with the facilitators, detailed medical information and medical records from the patient's doctor in the United States will be requested. Ideally, this information would be reviewed by a staff with a medical background before a foreign hospital and doctor are recommended. At a minimum, a facilitator should have a US board-certified physician review the medical records before a recommendation for treatment is made and the price for the procedure quoted. The board-certified physician can be sourced by the facilitator within or outside the United States. Interestingly, it is common for some US physicians to earn licenses in more than one country, thus allowing them to have hospital admitting privileges in more than one country.

Stamp of Approval

Certain website features are more inclined to improve a site's perceived credibility, for instance, if a firm's physical address is available on the website, or display of a privacy policy, or display of third-party endorsements like the logos of the Better Business Bureau (BBB), or ISO, or The Health on the Net Foundation (HON). The most common stamp of approval is, by far, the BBB. Some facilitators display the BBB logo on their websites to signal quality to the consumers. Membership in the BBB by itself does nothing to improve quality. However, less-established firms are less likely to become members because of the costs of the BBB's complaint resolution process. The BBB is an American nonprofit organization that monitors complaints against its member businesses, offers a dispute settlement service, makes complaint information available, and rates members on their complaint history. It has a special certification for Internet businesses. Facilitators often use quality indicators such as logos of the BBB, the ISO, or the accreditation agencies to raise consumers' perceptions of the firm's quality and trustworthiness. Studies have identified third-party endorsements, reputation, and brand recognition as vital elements in consumers building trust with companies on the Internet.

Industry Accreditation Standards and Certification

A study reviewing the facilitators' websites shows that 18 percent of the facilitators displayed Medical Tourism Association (MTA) logos, reflecting their certification or membership with the MTA, 5 percent displayed BBB logos, and 12 percent other logos, such as the HON (Health on the Net) logo and the ISQua seal (Gan & Frederick, 2015). In the same study, when it comes to hospital accreditation, 20 percent of facilitators displayed Joint Commission International JCI logos of hospitals to which they refer patients, with 15 percent claiming to refer exclusively to JCI-accredited hospitals. Only 6 percent of facilitators displayed accreditation logos based in other countries, such as the QHA Trent Accreditation, Accreditation Canada, the Australian Council for Healthcare Standards International, and other accreditation systems of the local governments.

All these accreditation standards imply the approval of objective and independent agencies. However, shockingly, only a few facilitators display these logos to lend credibility to their business and hospital recommendations. Some organizations certify facilitators, such as the Global Healthcare Accreditation, Temos International GmbH, the Medical Travel Quality Alliance, and Treatment Abroad's Code of Practice. Certification from some organizations can be costly, and satisfying their standards can be demanding. However, some systems are little more than membership organizations. Additionally, the HON code symbol indicates that a website follows HON standards. However, HON needs to verify the accuracy of the information on websites.

Furthermore, more than 50 percent of the facilitators reviewed in the same study displayed what are claimed to be patient testimonials (Gan & Frederick, 2015). Unfortunately, these can be obtained selectively and with little cost. Potential medical tourists should be aware of and skeptical of such testimonials. Sadly, many of the facilitators offered patient testimonials. However, few have obtained facilitator certifications or even mentioned hospitals' accreditations.

In a study based on seventeen Canadian facilitators' websites, the authors studied how the facilitators communicate risks and informed consent to their consumers (Penney et al., 2011). They found that most of the websites reviewed mentioned the agents' role in post-care, their prices, and treatment recovery time, some even mentioning third-party accreditation bodies. However, they often fell short of informing consumers of potential surgical risks. The information could have been more extensive and included on their websites.

The medical tourism market may be sustainable, but not all the stakeholders are as resilient as most would think. In how they operate, we expect to see a "shake-out" period in the medical tourism facilitator industry. The Covid-19 pandemic of 2020–2 has inadvertently expedited this process. The pandemic resulted in a 74 percent decline in global tourism in 2020, or one billion fewer international arrivals in 2020 than in 2019 (United Nations World Tourism Organization, 2021). The Covid-19 pandemic has wholly transformed the medical tourism industry, as the market requires traveling outside the country for medical treatment. The transactions in the medical tourism market have been adversely affected by travel restraints, preventing consumers of advanced economies from traveling to hospitals in destination countries, most of which are low to middle-income economies.

A recent website review of the facilitator market by the author shows that out of the 173 companies that existed in 2013, only fifty-one (33 percent) were still around in July 2020, soon after the Covid-19 pandemic had begun (Gan, 2020). Of the remaining 67 percent, the non-surviving companies, 67 percent of their original website domains were no longer available, 22 percent were put up for sale, and 11 percent had switched to other businesses.

During the pandemic years of 2020–2, some facilitators began marketing to domestic consumers, especially around health and wellness tourism. Wellness tourism includes spa services such as yoga, massage, acupuncture, Ayurveda, aromatic and herbal therapies, thermal springs, birdwatching, ecotourism, and agro-tourism. The new focus is expected to grow and remain in high demand post-Covid-19, domestically or internationally. This niche market will help drive the mainstream medical tourism market for at least the next five years.

In the long run, due to both pricing and non-pricing competition, the quality of service offered by the facilitators is expected to become more uniform, some niches, such as wellness tourism, will persist, and economic profit will diminish. There will be a need for a more robust industry-support model on international standards and patient protection beyond the efforts already put out by some of these facilitators' accreditation organizations, such as Global Healthcare Accreditation and Temos International GmbH. A list of current facilitators can be found on the website of Medical Tourism Research Center (www.uncp.edu/mtrc).

6

Interstate Medical Tourism in the United States

In this chapter, we will introduce the topic of interstate medical tourism. Interstate medical tourism is defined as traveling patients across state lines in the United States to seek medical treatment. There are various reasons why patients leave their home states to go to another state for medical services. It may be the unavailability of specialized treatments such as innovative cancer treatment or in vitro fertilization (IVF) service in their home states. It can even be non-approved procedures or remedies such as abortion or the use of cannabis for medicinal purposes. In this chapter, we will introduce interstate medical tourism by popular procedures, whether conventional or alternative medicine, sought by domestic medical tourists within the United States. We will also discuss why these procedures or products may be controversial, who the interstate medical tourists are, and what motivates them to travel.

Treatment Types

It is not uncommon for patients who seek more advanced and specialized treatments in cancer to travel to more reputable treatment centers in the United States, such as MD Anderson Center, Sloan Memorial Kettering Cancer Center, Harvard Medical Center, Johns Hopkins Hospital, or Mayo Clinic. For instance, James Allison, who shared the 2018 Nobel Prize with Tasuku Honjo, currently uses immunotherapy to treat cancer at MD Anderson Center. In recent decades, thousands of international and domestic patients have flocked to the center. Some American cancer patients would take the time and monetary effort to travel across state lines to such centers to receive specialized treatment.

It is estimated that $15 billion in revenue leaves the United States annually as Americans travel offshore for care, mainly for affordable elective treatments

(Sherwood, 2014). US states are working to lure those patients back by ramping up their quality of care, competitive pricing, and first-class facilities. Several Midwestern hospitals, notably those in Kansas City and Oklahoma City, have been seeking to attract patients from other states with prices significantly lower than what patients would pay in their home cities (Lytel, 2012). In 2014, Florida's legislature allocated $5 million to medical tourism, with half of the money set aside to promote Florida as a destination for patients and medical meetings. Rhode Island recently also enacted legislation to facilitate domestic medical tourism companies to set up business in the state. In 2013, Minnesota's legislature approved $585 million in funding to upgrade infrastructure in Rochester as part of Destination Medical Center, alongside Mayo Clinic's $5 billion expansion to "secure Minnesota's status as a global medical destination center" (Sherwood, 2014).

Further, the rising cost of health care has made many self-insured employers consider medical tourism a feasible option in their cost containment strategies. More employers are adding interstate medical tourism benefits to their health insurance. These employers include Wal-Mart, Boeing, Pepsi, and Lowe's. For instance, Lowe's allows their employees and dependents nationwide access to Cleveland Clinic, where they receive domestic medical tourism procedures (Medical Tourism Magazine, 2014). Walmart also contracts nationwide healthcare coverage with centers of excellence that perform heart, spine, and transplant surgeries.

Even though interstate medical tourism usually frames around traveling to centers of excellence. Increasingly, non-approved procedures or remedies such as IVF, abortion, or the use of medical cannabis are the other driving forces behind interstate medical tourism. In this case, engaging in tourism may or may not be relevant as it is not the primary purpose for travel. However, in the case of seeking medical cannabis, one may argue that potential patients may take time off for sightseeing because relaxation and nature are widely believed to be an alternative and holistic way to enhance one's healing process, as embraced by those who practice the complementary and alternative medicine (CAM).

Controversial Treatment

In Chapter 2, we discussed the unavailability of a particular treatment as the push or pull factor behind the use of medical tourism, albeit some controversial treatments such as stem cell therapy, organ transplantations, IVF, abortions, and the use of cannabis for medicinal purposes. Not all such treatments require crossing the country border; in the case of accessibility to abortion, IVF, or the use of medical cannabis, it may just be a matter of crossing the state lines to receive the procedure or product. Since we have already discussed stem cell therapy, organ transplantations, and the related controversies surrounding them in some detail in Chapter 2, in this chapter, we will focus mainly on reproductive tourism and its associated issues and, in a later section, the use of cannabis for medicinal purposes.

Abortion

The first reproductive tourism we will discuss is abortion. In the United States, abortion tops the list of other controversial issues, such as having a baby outside marriage, sex between teenagers, smoking marijuana, gay or lesbian relations, stem research using human embryos, and physician-assisted suicide.

Abortion is a huge political and dividing topic in the United States. All political figures running for office are being scrutinized closely where they stand on this topic. Indeed, voters have the right to know where these politicians stand on the issue and decide whether to vote for them. According to the Pew Research Center, the number of legally induced abortions performed in the United States declined around 1990. Over 93 percent of abortions occurred at or before thirteen weeks. The majority (57 percent) of women getting abortions are in their twenties, according to the Centers for Disease Control and Prevention (Kortsmit et al., 2022). Since the Supreme Court overturned *Roe v. Wade* (aka *the Dobbs decision*), or the ending of the Federal constitutional right to abortion in June of 2022, thus returning discretion over the legality of abortion to the states, more than a dozen states have banned abortion altogether, and more states are following suit. Despite the Supreme Court's ruling in 2022, there were still approximately 1.03 million abortions performed in the United States in 2023, as compared to a total of 930,000 abortions in 2020 (Maddow-Zimet & Gibson, 2024). One possible explanation is that the loss of access in states with bans has been offset by unprecedented efforts on the part of clinics, abortion funds, and logistical support organizations to help those in banned states access care through financial and practical support.

Why Controversial?

There are two dividing views when it comes to abortion. The pro-life view considers the fetus as a human being with complete moral rights since conception, thus regarding abortion as an act of killing. The pro-choice view, on the other end, regards the fetus as having no right or even intruding on women's rights to decide about their bodies or their families. Most Americans seem to hold views that fall somewhere in the middle.

In a Gallup report on where Americans stand on abortion, most Americans believe abortion should be legal to some degree (51percent), especially in the first trimester (69 percent) (Gallup, 2023a). The majority (61 percent) also disagree with the Supreme Court's overturning *Roe v. Wade*. In the same survey, the majority think second- (55 percent) and third-trimester abortions (70 percent) should generally be illegal. By age group, not surprisingly, 48 percent of US adults aged eighteen and twenty-nine held that abortion should be legal under any circumstances, as compared to 36 percent of those aged thirty and forty-nine and 27 percent of those fifty years old and above. As can be seen, these views are rather diverse by pregnancy trimester or by age group.

Who Are the Medical Tourists, and What Motivates Them?

The medical tourists in search of abortions are women of childbearing age who are faced with fetuses that are either unwanted, illegitimate, or disabled. Their motivation for abortion may be less than obvious. They may be seeking abortions based on unusual circumstances such as rape, incest, or complications in pregnancy that may lead to a life-threatening medical emergency. The laws governing these circumstances by which abortion is permitted vary widely from state to state.

Since the Supreme Court's *Dobbs decision* that revoked the federal right to abortion in June of 2022, with total bans from at least fourteen states, many reproductive health clinics have since shut down, and healthcare facilities and physicians who used to perform abortions have stopped. At the same time, some states have strengthened abortion rights, and new reproductive clinics have opened, with some of them strategically located in cities that border states with abortion bans. One of the interesting questions that has surfaced is where and how far women from states with abortion bans have to travel to access the procedure.

The proportion of American women who were situated more than 200 miles away from the closest abortion facility has increased dramatically. This occurred following the Supreme Court's ruling in June 2022. The percentage grew from 1 percent in April 2022 to 14 percent in April 2023 (Simmons-Duffin & Cheng, 2023). Likewise, the average distance from the provider for an average American woman has increased from 25 to 86 miles during the same period. Distance often prevents access to the providers, especially for lower-income women. They frequently face issues such as childcare, a lack of financial means to travel, inability to take time off work, or inability to lose wages.

It may come as a surprise to some that nearly two-thirds of all abortions in the United States in 2023 were medication abortions. The use of medication abortion has grown tremendously over the past two decades. In 2000, it accounted for less than 10 percent of all abortions in the United States. By 2020, this number had risen to 53 percent, and by 2023, it had reached 63 percent (Guttmacher Institute, 2024). This may be attributed to better access to telehealth in recent years. However, some think the actual figures may be higher if they also consider activities outside the formal healthcare system, such as obtaining the medication from a friend or over the counter at a pharmacy in Mexico.

Medication abortion is a method by which pregnancy is terminated by taking pills such as mifepristone or misoprostol. As of this writing, there are legal ambiguities surrounding mifepristone. A Texan judge ruled that the Food and Drug Administration (FDA) had improperly approved this drug. In contrast, another judge in Washington ruled that the FDA must continue to ensure public access to the drug. If the Texas case prevails, it can lead to a significant number of reproductive clinics closing and further limiting abortion access, especially in states that currently have high levels of access, such as California. In California, many abortion facilities only provide medication but not procedural abortions. In contrast, Maine is one of the states in which access to abortion has been broadened in recent years. Through telehealth, the state allows abortion pills to be prescribed without a patient seeing a doctor in person. In 2019, Maine authorized licensed allopathic or osteopathic physicians, physician assistants, and advanced practice registered nurses to provide abortion care services. An abortion law passed recently in Kentucky includes some new protocols for dispensing abortion pills and a provision to extradite people from other states who offer abortion pills to Kentuckians illegally (Totenberg & McCammon, 2022). Because of that, we can see why some state lawmakers, such as in Connecticut, are passing legislation to protect abortion providers from out-of-state lawsuits.

Where do the Americans stand on medication abortion? According to a recent *Gallup News*, 63 percent of US adults favored having mifepristone available in the United States with a prescription (Younis, 2023). By age group, 68 percent of those aged between eighteen and thirty-four supported its prescription use, compared to 61 percent support from those aged fifty-five and above. When the pill was first approved by the FDA in 2000, most Americans (50 percent) supported the decision, and 44 percent opposed it (Younis, 2023). However, earlier in 2000, a survey found more Americans opposed (47 percent) than in favor (39 percent) of making the drug available by prescription. Such dividing views explain why abortion and even the use of its medication continue to be controversial issues in the United States.

In Vitro Fertilization (IVF) Treatment

What do Elon Musk, the tech mogul, and Michael Jackson, the king of pop, have in common? They both have used in vitro fertilization (IVF) to have children. The second reproductive tourism we will discuss is IVF treatment. In 2023, 42 percent of Americans said they or someone they know had used some form of fertility treatment, a rise from 33 percent since 2018 (Goddard & Aragao, 2023). The white (48 percent) and Asian adults (45 percent) were the most inclined to say so; likewise, the upper-income group is much more likely than the middle-income group and below to say so. The result is to be expected, as fertility treatments can be costly. For instance, one cycle of in vitro fertilization can cost approximately $20,000 to $25,000. They are not usually covered by insurance. In the same 2023 survey, an estimated 10 percent of childbearing-age women (fifteen to forty-four years old) in the United States said they had received some form of fertility treatment. Older women between thirty-five and forty-four years old were more likely than those thirty-five years and below to receive these services. The most used service was fertility advice (78 percent), followed by fertility testing (61 percent), the use of drugs to improve ovulation (43 percent), artificial insemination (14 percent), surgery or used drugs to resolve tube blockages (11 percent), and IVF (2 percent). Although IVF is not the most used service, it has received the most public attention due to its controversies.

The Procedure

In vitro fertilization (IVF) is one of the most popular routes for American couples who struggle with infertility. IVF is a multistep procedure that involves combining human eggs and sperm outside of the body, usually in a clinical lab. A female first receives injectable hormones to spur her ovaries to grow mature eggs. The eggs were then removed from the ovaries and fertilized with sperm in a lab. The fertilized embryo is given a few days to develop and stabilize before implanted into a female uterus. It takes four to six weeks to complete the whole process.

Why Controversial?

Fertility treatment such as IVF is deemed controversial, and it sparks debates from ethical, religious, and legal standpoints. One argument says IVF goes against natural conception; for instance, a postmenopausal woman can still have a baby. Another criticism comes from an opposition to children being born to unmarried or same-sex couples. Yet another argues that a newborn child needs both a father and mother figure for healthy development. Catholic churches oppose IVF because they believe that infertility may be God's will. If so, one should not go against it. Other religions share the same belief. Others criticize the number of embryos involved in the procedures. In the IVF process, multiple embryos are customarily produced, fertilized, and then implanted into the uterus, with many discarded if they are of inferior quality to ensure a healthy chance of pregnancy. To some religious groups, each embryo represents life, so the disposal of embryos is treated in the same vein as abortion.

Who Are the Medical Tourists, and What Motivates Them?

According to the Centers for Disease Control and Prevention (CDC), 19 percent of women in the United States aged fifteen to forty-nine who have not had children were unable to get pregnant after trying for a year. Additionally, 26 percent of this group had issues with getting pregnant or carrying the pregnancy to full term (Centers for Disease Control and Prevention, 2024a). In 2017, about 41 percent of IVF procedures in the United States resulted in live births among women aged thirty-five to thirty-seven. However, the success rate dropped to 13 percent for older women aged forty-one to forty-two (Society for Assisted Reproductive Technology, 2017). In general, the Americans who travel for fertility treatment tend to be couples who are infertile, older women between thirty-five and forty-four years who are trying to get pregnant, or unmarried or same-sex couples. Other factors, such as obesity and STDs, can also contribute to the demand for such assisted reproductive technologies.

Cost is another significant factor, as the same IVF procedure can cost substantially less if couples are willing to travel outside their state or the country. Even though twenty-one states in the United States plus Washington, DC, have passed fertility insurance coverage laws, with sixteen of the states including some form of mandated IVF coverage and seventeen of them covering fertility preservation for iatrogenic (or medically induced) infertility, there are variations in coverage. For instance, California law does not include IVF. As mentioned, one IVF cycle may run approximately $20,000 to $25,000. Thus, American couples have every reason to shop and cross the state or country border for a cheaper alternative, especially those who reside outside those twenty-one states.

Inducement by third-party payers is another essential motivation to seek IVF. As of June 2022, twenty states in the United States required insurance companies to offer coverage for fertility treatment, including IVF. Companies increasingly provide these options to their employees for the remaining states with no mandatory coverage. These companies include Cisco, MassMutual, Chobani, and Starbucks, with the latter even offering these benefits to their hourly workers. Technology giants such as Apple, Facebook, and Microsoft extended the benefits beyond the basics, covering egg harvesting and freezing services (Leonhardt, 2019). A recent study showed that 40 percent of organizations in the United States have included fertility benefits in their 2023 benefits packages—an improvement from 30 percent of US companies in 2020 (Wellable, 2023).

Timing is another solid motivation for travel as the success rate with IVF technologies declines with an increase in childbearing age. Waiting time in some countries can exceed twelve months. Therefore, some choose to seek timely and affordable care in another country. In other instances, patients from developing countries who can afford it may choose to access a higher quality of services or expertise in developed countries such as the United States. In addition to the United States, other top country destinations for IVF treatment are Spain, Portugal, Greece, North Cyprus, Denmark, Latvia, Poland, Czech Republic, Jordan, Mexico, and Barbados.

Gender Selection

One of the popular motivations to seek IVF is gender selection, which is another controversial subtopic by itself, as some countries or states in the United States ban the practice. Some patients will travel to Belgium, Finland, Greece, India, or some states in the United States where gender selection is not illegal. Many patients from all over the world are choosing the United States as their preferred destination for IVF, not only for gender selection but also for commercial surrogacy (which is legal in states like California and Minnesota), anonymous sperm donation, and, as bizarre as it may sound, the ability to screen for physical characteristics such as eye color (Cha, 2018).

There is much debate on the morality of so-called designer babies as scientists found ways to experiment with gene editing. Concerns are raised over the increase in the screening of embryos for characteristics such as intelligence, physical appearance, and gender. These procedures raised similar ethical questions about manipulating human reproduction.

Gender selection is possible in IVF through a process known as preimplantation genetic diagnosis (PGD). In the process, a single cell or a few cells are taken from the embryo to examine its genetic makeup using DNA probes. In addition to screening embryos for inherited diseases, which is usually done, PGD can also be used to identify embryos with specific desirable characteristics by the parents (Cha, 2018). To be clear, PGD does not change the embryo, but it helps potential parents select which embryos to transfer to the womb and which to dispose of.

Some European countries ban the use of PGD for elective gender selection. However, the United States does not regulate PGD nor limit its use to specific indications. Statistics on gender selection are sparse. A 2006 survey by Johns Hopkins University found that 42 percent of American fertility clinics offered PGD for gender selection (Sidhu, 2012). A more recent 2018 survey found that nearly 73 percent of US fertility clinics offered gender selection (Capelouto et al., 2018). Of those clinics, 84 percent provided it to couples who do not have fertility problems but are considering IVF sorely to control the pregnancy's outcome. The United States has become a popular destination for wealthy fertility patients from around the world, particularly those from China, where gender selection is banned. International organizations such as Gender Selection Australia send thousands of patients yearly to American IVF clinics to take advantage of the service (Cha, 2018).

Lately, other countries have been restricting their regulations on reproductive tourism. In 2017, India banned commercial surrogacy. In 2019, Ireland joined Finland, Norway, Sweden, Switzerland, the Netherlands, New Zealand, and others in prohibiting anonymous sperm donation. Moreover, a host of countries, including China, Canada, and Australia, ban gender selection except in cases of "necessary medical need."

Use of Medical Cannabis

Marijuana, which is also known as "cannabis," "hemp," or "weed," is the most used federally illegal drug in the United States, with an estimated fifty-three million or 19 percent of Americans using it in 2021(Centers for Disease Control and Prevention, 2024b). As of February 2024, cannabis is legal in the United States in some form and for different purposes except in six states (Idaho, Kansas, Nebraska, North Carolina, South Carolina, and Wyoming). Although it is still illegal federally, it has been recreationally or medicinally used by about half of all Americans. As of 2023, it is also medicinally and recreationally legal in countries such as Belize, Canada, Columbia, Czech Republic, Netherlands, Spain, and Uruguay.

Why Controversial?

When it comes to medical cannabis, some argue that smoked cannabis is more effective than conventional treatment in finding a cure or reliving patients' health symptoms. However, some say that the smoke from cannabis is toxic. It could open the door to the abuse of harder drugs such as cocaine and heroin, and it could also convey the wrong message that the use of illegal drugs is safe.

Who Are the Medical Tourists, and What Motivates Them?

According to a 2022 study by the Pew Research Center, a large proportion of US adults (88 percent) favor the legalization of cannabis, either for both medicinal and recreational use (59 percent) or for medicinal use only (30 percent) (Green, 2022). This is up from 70 percent in favor of both purposes in 2018 (Blake, 2018) and up from 48 percent for both purposes in 2015. In the same 2022 study, the support for cannabis legalization is incredibly overwhelming among young people, with 72 percent in favor among those ages eighteen to twenty-nine and 62 percent among those ages thirty to forty-nine. For older age groups, approximately 54 percent of those ages fifty to seventy-four and 30 percent of those seventy-five years old and above are in favor of the legalization of cannabis. These statistics by age are to be expected.

However, there seems to be a reversal in age when it comes to the use of *medical* cannabis in the United States, according to the National Survey on Drug Use and Health (Public Health Institute, 2023). It is the age group of sixty-five or older who were experimenting with the use of medical cannabis more than other age groups. The figure has tripled from 11 percent to 35 percent between 2009 and 2021. Even in the slightly younger age group of sixty to sixty-four, more than 50 percent had reported the use of cannabis. The new trend is driven mainly by a combination of physical illnesses, the increased cultural acceptance of cannabis, and the marketing efforts to promote cannabis as a therapeutic agent. As nationwide legalization and opening of dispensaries have reduced the stigma attached to the recreational drug in recent years, an increasing number of older Americans are experimenting with the drug for more practical reasons such as sleep aids and pain management.

Use of Cannabis for Medicinal Purposes

Cannabis has more than 100 compounds, including tetrahydrocannabinol (THC) and cannabidiol (CBD). THC can be "mind-altering," whereas CBD does not cause a "high." Various states offer products with different ratios of these compounds. Some medical programs offer 20-to-1 ratios or even 5-to-1 ratios of different CBD and THC combinations. In addition to being anticancer, THC is medically beneficial in the treatments of Alzheimer's, anxiety, arthritis, chemotherapy side effects, Crohn's disease, chronic pain, fibromyalgia, incontinence, insomnia, Lou Gehrig's disease, and sleep apnea (United Patients Group, 2024). On the other hand, CBD can help balance adrenals and modulate hormone production and release, especially in stress response. The benefits of CBD include helping to stop the spread of cancer cells, depression, diabetes, epilepsy, inflammation, mood disorders, multiple sclerosis, and neuropathic pain (United Patients Group, 2024).

In several states in the United States (Georgia, Indiana, Iowa, Kentucky, Tennessee, Texas, and Wisconsin), only CBD oil is permitted for medicinal purposes. CBD oil is a natural ingredient of the cannabis plant, and its transactions are becoming increasingly popular. It may be sold as an oil containing only one active ingredient or as a hemp plant extract in oil. It may be sold in capsules, as dried cannabis, or as a prescription liquid.

Regarding nutrition, hemp seeds and hemp oil, which are sold legally in grocery stores, are packed with omega 3 fatty acids, clean protein, and other vital nutrients. According to Bollinger, the author of *The truth about cancer*, "Phoenix Tears" is one of the most promising cannabis varietals for treating cancer. It was rediscovered by Rick Simpson, who successfully used the oil to cure his basal cell carcinoma (Bollinger, 2016, p. 174). Since then, many medical dispensaries have started manufacturing and selling the product directly to patients. Bollinger also told the success story of Trevor Smith from London, who was diagnosed with stage T2A bladder cancer in 2012 but successfully overcame the illness by taking high doses of highly concentrated cannabis oil (Bollinger, 2016, p. 175). He also did a complete dietary overhaul, eating no processed foods and consuming plenty of organic chicken, vegetables, nuts and seeds, and fresh juices. These natural treatments eventually helped him become completely cancer-free, even after being told he would never survive without taking chemotherapy and radiation. Bollinger concluded that a combination of a diet change, various vitamins, hemp oil, and keeping a positive mental attitude were keys to Trevor's victory over cancer.

At the home front, in the state of Virginia, Helmer's bill was passed to approve public sector employees to use cannabis products to treat medical conditions. Joe Mirabile, who represents Virginia's Professional Firefighters, in his support for the bill in a committee hearing, testified that "my members have reported that they are relying on alcohol far less, they are sleeping more at home, and they are seeing other positive effects, such as reduction of joint and muscle pain without having to use opioid prescription" (Chun, 2024).

Despite skepticism by the US Centers for Disease Control and Prevention, there was conclusive or significant evidence that cannabis is effective for treating cancer-related pain, chemotherapy-induced nausea and vomiting, and spasticity in multiple sclerosis. It is also helpful in treating anorexia, post-traumatic stress disorder (PTSD), insomnia, anxiety, and depression. In Israel, for instance, cannabis in various forms is being overwhelmingly administered by the pediatric oncology department at Hadassah Hospital in Jerusalem. In the Netherlands, a country with the most extended history of cannabis use, both recreational and medicinal, physicians have been able to prescribe medical cannabis for their patients since 2003. In Italy, patients could freely obtain cannabis prescriptions from their primary care physicians since 2014. Medical cannabis has also been legalized in other European countries, such as France, Romania, and the Czech Republic. The use of Sativex has been approved in at least seventeen European countries (Bifulco & Pisanti, 2015). Lebanon became the first country in the Middle East to legalize cannabis for medicinal and industrial purposes in 2020.

Interstate Commerce Issues

As of April 2023, thirty-eight states, three territories, and the District of Columbia have allowed the use of medical cannabis products (National Conference of State Legislatures, 2023). Moreover, as of November of 2023, the same source also revealed that two territories and the District of Columbia have enacted measures to regulate cannabis for recreational use. Various state regulations on these issues have complicated the interstate commerce of cannabis. Some of the main problems certain states face are highlighted in the following section.

California, Oregon, Washington

The West Coast dominated cannabis production in the nation long before state legalization. California has long been plagued with an oversupply of cannabis by struggling cannabis farmers. The vast surplus of cannabis remains officially trapped within each state's borders due to the federal ban on cannabis.

Prices have dropped drastically, and producers have struggled. California is working on enacting a law that will allow the exporting of cannabis goods to other states. In Oregon, cannabis sales began in 2015, and large growers have achieved economies of scale that could give them an advantage in a broader market. However, the oversupply of cannabis is considered the nation's worst. In February of 2023, it was reported that businesses were sitting on 3 million pounds of unused cannabis and 75,000 pounds of concentrates and extracts (Johnson, Selsky, & Blood, 2023). One reason behind the excess supply in Oregon and, to a lesser extent, in Washington was that too many licenses were issued to farmers. The initial intention was to ensure plenty of supply for the legal market, bringing down prices to compete with the black market. With over half of Washington's population, Oregon has a hundred more licensed growers than Washington state.

In Washington, the state's 37 percent cannabis tax is one of the highest cannabis taxes in the country; the prices the consumers pay in the retail store are still cheaper than illicit weed. In fact, in 2021, at least three-quarters of cannabis users in the states of Washington, Oregon, and Colorado reported they bought cannabis products from legal retail outlets. On the one hand, consumers pay as little as $100 to $150 per pound of cannabis in 2023 as compared to $3,000 when legal sales began in Oregon in 2015 (Johnson, Selsky, and Blood, 2023). On the other hand, the state's 37 percent cannabis tax leaves virtually no profit margins for the producers. The low prices and low-profit margins make the industry hardly sustainable. This leads to two possible outcomes—entering interstate commerce or resorting to illicit market sales.

In March 2023, Washington's lawmakers approved a "trigger bill" similar to the ones already passed in California and Oregon. The bill authorized the governor to enter interstate cannabis trade agreements should the Federal government permit it. Washington and Colorado were the first states to legalize recreational marijuana in 2012. Since the beginning, Washington has adopted restricting the size of growing facilities and banning out-of-state investment. That has helped smaller farmers to thrive. However, it could hamstring those hoping to compete in an interstate marketplace along with larger and more efficient growers from California and Oregon, who operate under fewer limits.

A second unintended spill-over problem these states face is the growth of the black market or illegal sales. The arrival of legal sales in California in 2018 was seen as a breakthrough that opened the door for federal legalization. However, two-thirds of California communities do not allow legal cannabis activities, which helps the tax-free illegal market to flourish. Los Angeles alone has only around

350 legal retail stores compared to twice or thrice the number of illicit stores and delivery services (Elinson & Vielkind, 2023). As in Oregon, California growers have pushed legal products into illegal sales. It was reported that California's legal market lost nearly one-quarter of its total growing area at the beginning of 2022. In 2022, legal sales in California totaled only $5.4 billion, compared to illegal sales of $8.1 billion (Elinson & Vielkind, 2023). Legal cannabis businesses, with their higher prices and higher taxes, were hit the hardest in California. Curaleaf, based in New York and offers vaporizer cartridges, pre-rolled joints, and a variety of other products, laid off 200 employees in November of 2022 and announced in early 2023 that it was closing its locations in California, Oregon, and Colorado. In contrast, states such as Nevada and Arizona have done a better job in curbing the illicit market and were able to strike the right balance between growers and retail stores. Nevada legalized cannabis possession in 2016, and 74 percent of the products have been sold through legal channels. According to New Frontier Data, Arizona was legalized in 2020, and 55 percent has been sold legally (Elinson & Vielkind, 2023).

North Carolina

As of 2024, cannabis is still a controlled substance in North Carolina, and possession of it is illegal. The penalty for possessing cannabis depends on the type, how much one has, and how one plans to use it. One can possess up to 1.5 ounces of cannabis for personal use and up to 0.15 ounces of hash or concentrates. The 2018 Farm Bill said that hemp is no longer a controlled substance and can be grown as a regular crop. All hemp-derived products, including CBD, are legal in the state as long as they contain less than 0.3 percent delta-9 THC. The federally legal alternative for cannabis, known as delta-8 THC, is the only legal cannabis product in the state as long as it contains less than 0.3 percent delta-9 THC. Delta-8 THC is found in trace quantities in cannabis and can be distilled and synthesized from hemp. It is increasingly being marketed as medical cannabis with less of the "high" and anxiety (Grinspoon, 2022). Delta-8 THC can be found easily in the state's local hemp stores and online. On April 20, 2024, a significant day for marijuana stakeholders, the state's first dispensary for medical marijuana was opened on Cherokee Indian tribal land in the Great Smoky Mountain.

Kentucky

Starting in the year 2023, individuals with severe medical conditions in Kentucky who fulfill specific criteria will be permitted to hold and consume small quantities of medical cannabis that they have legally acquired. As there is no medical marijuana law in effect in the state, there are presently no medical marijuana dispensaries operating in Kentucky. The Kentuckians will have to travel to buy from other states. Ohio has such dispensaries, but they cannot sell to out-of-state residents. That means Kentuckians whom their doctors approve will have to drive to states such as Michigan or Illinois, where they can buy cannabis recreationally (Knef, 2022). That comes with its problems.

District of Columbia (DC) and Maryland

Although recreational consumption is legal in both jurisdictions, the laws for the possession and sale of cannabis and even its cultivation vary in each. Cannabis users traveling across the states should bear in mind that it is illegal to transport cannabis over state lines, and the drug remains illegal on federal property.

In the District of Columbia (DC), it is legal for adults to possess up to two ounces of cannabis and cultivate up to six cannabis plants in their homes. However, the consumption of cannabis is only allowed on private property. Although recreational cannabis was approved in 2015, the sale of the drug remains a gray market. Enterprising shops in DC have developed a gifting system whereby they sell unrelated goods, such as a T-shirt or herbal tea, and offer a small amount of cannabis as a gift with the purchase (Shepherd, 2023). While the workaround may be legal, local officials maintain that it is illegal to sell any amount of recreational cannabis to another person. In contrast, the sales of medical cannabis are legal for up to eight ounces in thirty days. DC's legal medical market has become more accessible since March of 2023 when the Medical Cannabis Amendment Act allows patients to self-certify that they have a qualifying medical condition without a doctor's note. There is a 6 percent sales tax levied on the sales of medical cannabis in DC, and there is a tax holiday in April that waives the tax at licensed medical dispensaries.

Maryland law permits adults to buy and consume recreational cannabis legally. Within the state, delivery of marijuana is also allowed. Adults can possess up to 1.5 ounces of cannabis flower and a maximum of twelve grams of concentrated cannabis at any given time. It is legal to possess up to 750 mg of THC total in any combination of forms. They are allowed to grow up to two cannabis plants in their private home, out of public view. While the consumption of cannabis is limited to within the privately owned home, it is not legal to consume it inside a motor vehicle. There is a 9 percent sales tax levied on the sales of cannabis in Maryland.

By the end of December 2022, Maryland's medical program had served nearly 163,000 patients. As of March 2023, Washington, DC, had provided medical care to just under 30,000 unique DC resident patients and thousands of non-DC resident patients (VCU CNS, 2023). The DC-area medical dispensaries can sell to out-of-state residents, such as Virginians who have a certificate and a valid state ID.

Virginia

In Virginia, it is legal for adults to consume recreational cannabis. They are allowed to possess a maximum of one ounce of cannabis and cultivate a maximum of four plants if they are out of reach of children. Possessing more than one ounce but less than a pound of cannabis can result in a $25 civil fine in Virginia. Having more than one pound of the drug is a felony. Moreover, adults are allowed to give up to one ounce of cannabis to another adult. It is permitted to consume cannabis only on private property.

The sole legal option to purchase cannabis in Virginia is through the medical cannabis market. However, several ongoing concerns have been reported, such as expensive registration fees and high prices, inconsistent supply, low potency, and limited accessibility overall (VCU CNS, 2023). After an initial consultation, Virginia residents must first obtain a written certificate from a registered state practitioner. The certificate can cost as much as $100 and must be renewed annually. There are approximately 1,000 approved medical cannabis practitioners in Virginia (Chun, 2024). There are approximately seventeen dispensaries located in Virginia. A government-issued ID and certificate must be presented to make the first purchase. In 2023, a total of 98,000 patients used their written certificates to receive medical cannabis through the state program, according to the state managing agency Cannabis Control Authority. In Virginia, there were almost 562,000 dispensations of medical cannabis products in 2021, and the total grew to over 1.44 million in 2022 (VCU CNS, 2023).

There are a couple of concerns related to pricing and inconsistent product availability. It has been observed that products similar to the ones available at a dispensary in Virginia are being sold at a lesser price at the same company's dispensary in a different state. For example, a product that costs $60 in Virginia can cost $35 for the same amount in Philadelphia, that is, from the same parent company (VCU CNS, 2023). As such, some patients turn to the black market, hoping to get a better deal. However, black market products may be unsafe as they are not inspected for heavy metals, pesticides, or other contaminants that otherwise would be found through state-regulated testing.

To sum up, as cannabis is still considered illegal by the federal government, potential patients should bear in mind that insurance companies may decline to cover the purchase of medical cannabis and its referrals. Before traveling to another state, potential interstate medical tourists must do some research regarding state regulations on cannabis. On May 1, 2024, the Federal Drug Enforcement Agency (DEA) announced a landmark move to remove cannabis from the Schedule I drug list and relist it as a Schedule III drug. The implication of this historical move is enormous. We can expect to see more clinical trials and research being carried out on the therapeutic use of cannabis, endorsed and funded by pharmaceutical companies. This will eventually lead to the commercialization of cannabis drugs widely prescribed by conventional physicians and their acceptable use. It will not be long before they appear on the list of prescription drugs approved by the insurance companies and made available to the needful patients.

Part II

Issues and Controversies

7

Consumers' Concerns Related to Medical Tourism

Just as there are myriad motivations for medical tourists to travel abroad for care, there are numerous deterrents to them in this emerging industry. This chapter addresses consumers' concerns related to medical tourism. The fundamental question is which country and hospital to choose from and which facilitator if one is used. Many things can go wrong when traveling to a foreign country on a long flight, especially when patients need treatments. Continuity of care, potential medical negligence, and malpractice are legitimate issues for those contemplating medical tourism. Closely related to those is whether the destination hospitals are HIPAA compliant, thus ensuring the privacy protection of consumers' records. Fiduciary responsibility is another question that arises when sorting out whether insurers or facilitators are liable in cases of violation of HIPAA privacy law or medical malpractice. As discussed in Chapters 1, 6, and 9, there are regulatory and ethical issues that evolve around controversial treatments such as organ transplantation, fertility treatment, abortion, and the use of medical cannabis. The complexity of the problems can deter medical tourists from seeking those treatments abroad. Finally, one psychological hindrance is simply the perceptions of destination countries regarding medical needs, quality of care, and culture.

Choice of Healthcare Provider

There are various opinions on how a potential medical tourist would choose which country or hospital to go to. Suppose one does not utilize a medical tourism facilitator. In that case, one is likely to select the hospital first with some consideration of the destination country's potential tourism sites. Suppose the potential medical tourists decide to contact the destination hospitals directly. In that case, the former usually faces substantial asymmetric information. Most hospitals' information is limited to what is published on their website, which may include a virtual tour of the hospital facility, information on hospital accreditation or affiliation, treatment types and procedures, insurance information, and online reviews by previous patients. However, the info prospective patients seek sometimes goes beyond what is viewable on a hospital's website. From the potential patient's viewpoint, the two most important aspects are invariably the quality of care and the services provided by the hospital. We will explain this in the following section.

The strategic location of the hospital is a critical selection criterion for most medical tourists planning to travel to a particular country for the first time. They would prefer a hospital close to amenities like shopping, dining, and banking services, not in the middle of a crowded city center, and preferably near the airport. The quality of hospital services includes the availability of an international patient center, integrated billing, and partnerships with international insurers. As highlighted in a few hospital cases in Chapter 4, the fact that a hospital has an international patient center demonstrates its commitment to serving international patients. The center acts as a middleman without an agent and often takes care of essential concierge services for medical tourists. The center is usually equipped with multi-language staff. It deals exclusively with the needs of international patients, for instance, visa extension, meet and greet at the airport, and arranging sightseeing tours. If the hospital offers integrated billing, it is a big plus as patients can see the clear and transparent billing when they are discharged and leave the country. It is more efficient than the billing practice in most US hospitals, in which dozens of bills from various hospital departments will be mailed separately to patients weeks following the treatment. Finally, a strategic partnership with international insurance companies is a quality signal for hospital services because such a partnership requires good networking and negotiations with the insurers. The partnership makes insurance filing a seamless process for patients even before returning to their home countries.

In addition to international accreditation and reputation, the quality of care usually includes surgical outcomes, credentials and training of foreign doctors, low nurse–patient ratio, and advanced medical technology. The quality of care a foreign hospital provides is more complex to define because it is not as easily observable as certain tangible services the hospital offers. It is, therefore, strongly advisable for potential medical tourists to exercise due diligence and do their research before committing to any treatment in a particular foreign hospital. For instance, the doctors' credentials are usually not published on most hospital websites. Nevertheless, it is essential to research the facility and the doctor performing the procedure. While information about different facilities and doctors is easily accessible in the United States, potential patients will find it harder to access that information from destination hospitals outside the United States (Whitlock, 2020). Before officially agreeing to surgery, potential patients should research their surgeons' credentials. For instance, where they received their medical education, where they were trained, and what their area(s) of specialty are. Potential medical tourists should rely on more than just the opinions and reviews of others. Online reviews can be easily fabricated to make the facility or the doctor look better. Even if online reviews are authentic, one successful surgery does not necessarily mean all such surgeries yield similar outcomes. Different patients have diverse medical histories and preexisting conditions; they may not all be treated the same way.

It is also essential to learn about the country's healthcare system in general, specifically the environment and resources of the hospital. If complications occur during and after the surgeries, does the hospital have the resources, or will the patient need to be referred to a different facility? (Whitlock, 2020). Another complication that could arise is the post care. Suppose one plans to have one's follow-up care performed in the United States. In that case, it is wise to schedule that before leaving the country and let one's home doctor know where and from whom one will receive the procedure. Communication with one's home doctors is vital because most doctors in the United States hesitate to work with patients who have received care from another country. The reasons are that home doctors are unaware of the quality of work that has been performed, the unavailability of medical records, and the possibility of dealing with an impending malpractice suit.

As the market for medical tourism continues to grow, it is wise to do thorough research on the area one will be staying in, the area where the hospital is located, the hospital itself, and the physician or the team who will be performing the procedure and overseeing the healing process. It is also essential to ensure proper insurance and prearrange follow-up visits with a physician in the United States. With the right amount of preparation, medical tourism can be a safe and effective way to receive medical treatment at a lower rate than offered in the United States.

Choice of Facilitator

As mentioned in Chapter 1, due to asymmetric information and high search costs, an average potential medical tourist knows little about foreign countries and foreign hospitals' services. Therefore, one may prefer to hire a facilitator or agent. Choosing a provider becomes more manageable when a potential patient uses an agent, but is it true? Yes, the agents can do all the legwork and help the potential patients shortlist which hospital and destination county to seek care. However, the big question now becomes which facilitator to choose from.

As with foreign hospitals, potential medical tourists face a high degree of asymmetric information regarding facilitating firms. Moreover, like most foreign hospitals, information about the facilitators is limited to what is published on their websites, which varies considerably from one agent to another. There is basically little evidence of pricing transparency on most facilitators' websites and even very little information about the history of the company on the website, making it challenging for potential medical tourists to choose which one to use. Agents' services are like "experienced" services in the healthcare and travel business. As such, potential patients should choose an agent who strives to provide them with a positive experience from the beginning to the end of the journey.

In a 2008 study on medical tourism agents, some respondents cited features that affect their destination choice: the agents' reputation, accommodation, security and safety, and travel time (Legiewski & Myers, 2008). Some also cited concierge services in the destination countries and their related support contributing to their positive medical tourism experience. One source believes that the best facilitators provide potential patients with transparent pricing for travel coordination, including transfers and hotels. They also choose hospitals from their network based on accreditation, patient flow, nurse–patient ratios, quality improvement programs, staffing, and other performance-related activities.

Penney et al. (2011) studied how facilitators communicate risks and informed consent to their prospective patients in a study based on seventeen Canadian facilitators' websites. They found most of the websites reviewed mentioned the agents' role in post care, their prices, and treatment recovery time. Some even mentioned third-party accreditation bodies, but many fell short of informing patients of potential surgical risks. The information was either limited or missing on their websites.

Another study explored the benefits and risks featured on close to 100 non-US agents' websites and examined how they use various persuasive appeals to attract prospective patients (Lee et al., 2014). They found these websites stressed benefits while downplaying the risks. Even though they advertised complicated and risky treatments, no report of any procedural, post-care, or any related legal concerns was found on these sites.

Further, another study showed that a little more than 50 percent of the facilitators displayed what were claimed to be patient testimonials on their websites (Gan & Frederick, 2015). Unfortunately, these can be obtained selectively and with little cost. Potential medical tourists should be aware of and skeptical of such testimonials. All the information portrayed on the agents' websites sometimes does not adequately reflect the "quality of care" of the referring hospitals or the services provided by the agents. The best recommendation should come from satisfied friends and families who have successfully used a particular agent.

Finally, potential patients should keep in mind that during the pandemic years of 2020–2, most facilitators have either folded their businesses or shifted to niche markets such as wellness tourism. Potential patients should also know that the medical tourism agent's industry is self-regulated. As such, there are some potential problems and issues. As pointed out in Chapter 5, various organizations worldwide try to certify or "regulate" the industry. However, the current fragments of traditional medical tourism facilitators need a more robust industry support model on international standards and patient protection beyond the efforts already put forth by some of these self-declared accreditation organizations.

Cost Concerns

Although cost saving is one of the main reasons medical tourists travel to other countries for care, especially the uninsured and underinsured, it is not the only one. Potential patients need to watch out for some hidden costs. Continuity of care remains a legitimate issue for prospective patients who contemplate medical tourism. Some argue that complications, side effects, and postoperative care can defeat the cost-saving for those seeking care abroad. Patients may require additional treatment after returning to the United States, which the insurance may not cover. Potential medical tourists should exercise common sense by checking with their insurers for complete treatment coverage from the beginning through the post-care stage before planning a medical trip outside the country.

It is highly advisable to purchase separate travel insurance. However, even with good travel insurance, there are other potential financial risks due to limited coverage by travel insurance. Suppose complications develop during or after the procedure that require additional treatments. In that case, the patients may not be covered by their health insurance, let alone travel insurance. They may face significant emergency evacuation costs to their home countries if there are complications, and patients need to ensure their travel insurance covers this. While travel insurance is readily available, it is rare to find complications insurance. A few insurance companies offer complications insurance in the United States, as pointed out in Chapter 5. Some complications insurance waives all deductibles and coinsurance and covers between $15,000 and $50,000 (depending on the procedure) within a year after the complications have occurred (Medical Tourism Corporation, 2024). Some agents, such as Medical Tourism Corporation, offer "health travel insurance." It covers additional medical expenses related to complications, which include extra consultations and hospital stays and extra travel expenditures to the destination hospitals, such as airfare and accommodation for a maximum of one year. It is highly recommended for potential patients who plan to undergo significant surgeries abroad to purchase complications insurance and travel insurance and have peace of mind.

Perceptions and Cultural Differences

Some potential medical tourists may have certain perceptions of a destination country, especially if it is a developing or third-world country. Cheap health care in developing countries often evokes images of spaces that are not sanitized with doctors who may or may not have a medical degree. Some perceive that hospital staff in developing countries may not be highly aware of sanitation and that patients may be susceptible to severe disease infection from the hospital itself. These are unfavorable stereotypes; they may or may not be true.

Closely related to perceptions are cultural differences, another critical consideration for some medical tourists when determining which country to select. Cultural differences can include receiving care in an unfamiliar environment or the degree of fluency with which the patient's native language is spoken by hospital staff. Granted, one psychological hindrance in a cross-cultural setting is the strong affinity to one's familiar care environment regarding medical needs and quality of care (Carrera & Bridges, 2006). These medical needs could apply to various areas, including how the doctors communicate procedures, how the nurses provide care, how patients' concerns are being addressed, and whether the hospital staff complies with the American HIPAA or privacy protection law.

Further, most people in the destination country do not speak English or speak only limited English. In that case, patients are more inclined to feel anxious, isolated, and vulnerable because of poor communication, which may negatively affect their overall recovery. If the patients travel alone, there are other concerns, such as the stress involved in having treatments in a foreign country, away from the support of friends and family. As such, it is highly recommended that potential patients travel with at least a companion, be it a family member, friend, or caregiver.

Moreover, as far as hospital diets are concerned, many destination hospitals are usually more than willing to cater to special diets such as vegetarian, kosher, halal, or even certain ethnic diets. For instance, Muslim patients would prefer to travel to Malaysia, where they know the meals will be prepared in the "halal" way, that is, according to the Muslim code of food preparation. To cater to and attract their growing Middle Eastern patients, some South Korean hospitals have hired Arabic-speaking interpreters and trained their hospital cooks to prepare Middle Eastern meals. Potential medical tourists with diet concerns are advised to communicate with their destination hospitals in advance and ask for accommodations. Most destination hospitals are usually more than happy to meet the needs of potential medical tourists.

How would a potential medical tourist overcome problems related to country perception or cultural differences? Other than being open to slightly different ways of providing care in various countries, learning a new culture or even a language, and having the opportunity to visit rare sights in their lifetime, options are always available. Medical tourists will need to look hard and honestly reassess their tradeoffs. For instance, if cultural similarity is an important consideration, one may need to compromise treatment cost and choose a country that has a closer cultural similarity than America, such as Germany, Poland, Spain, or Portugal, even if it means incurring a higher overall cost.

Travel Concerns

Travel concerns relate to the destination county potential medical tourists travel to and the journey involved. Some concerns may be geopolitical, such as whether a country has a stable political and social environment and free from natural disasters, experiencing a new climate, or being exposed to new strains of virus, bacteria, or fungus infection while traveling. They go beyond just meeting the routine immunizations required by the destination countries. Regarding travel safety, potential patients should read the travel advisories published by the US

Department of State on its website (travel.state.gov) before making any medical travel plan to a particular country.

When considering which country to travel to, the further the distance, the longer the flight time. A long-haul flight of more than five hours can increase the risk of deep vein thrombosis or blood clots. Also, the longer the flight time, the harder it is for one to get over the jet lag after returning home. Further, some potential patients may be concerned with prolonged absenteeism from their work, assuming there will be additional pretesting before the surgery and a convalescent period before they are fit to travel home. All these should be factored in when choosing which destination country or hospital to seek care.

Patient Safety Concern

From the patients' viewpoint, in addition to cost savings and travel safety, they are most concerned with their clinical outcomes. Medical tourists may risk compromising their health safety while undergoing treatment in another country. For one, they may be exposed to antibiotic-resistant bacteria that can cause complications after surgery. They should check the Centers for Disease Control and Prevention's (CDC's) website for the latest report on surgery complications performed in certain facilities outside the United States.

Furthermore, there need to be a clear discussion between the patients and the foreign doctors concerning if the procedure is necessary. The foreign doctors are supposed to fully disclose to the patients the risks and any related side effects of the surgery so that the patients can make a fully informed decision. The patients should also enquire if there is any post-surgery follow-up to ensure satisfactory outcomes.

Moreover, the United States does not require its hospitals to measure and report surgical outcomes or participate in international performance-measurement systems. Therefore, it is not easy to compare relative quality with the destination hospital (Milstein & Smith, 2006). The main thing to watch out for is any problems that may surface in the post-care. Patients may face the risk of infection and unavailability of medical records regarding the procedure. A lack of continuity of care may require patients to seek a different doctor in the United States to fix the problem. However, because of difficulties in obtaining medical records and possible malpractice concerns, some US doctors may be reluctant to treat patients who have surgeries offshore.

Further, there are regulatory or ethical issues that evolve around controversial treatments, such as organ transplantation, stem cell, fertility treatment, and abortion, that can sometimes deter some from seeking such medical treatment abroad. These issues have been discussed in Chapters 1, 6, and 9; we will not repeat them here.

Privacy Concerns

When a potential medical tourist prefers greater privacy in treatment, traveling outside the country for care is ideal. That explains why cosmetic and bariatric surgeries are so popular outside the United States. For instance, they are popular in Mexico, Brazil, Peru, and Panama. Gender reassignment is another procedure that a potential patient would value for greater privacy.

The compliance of the American HIPAA law in destination hospitals and related issues concern all US traveling patients. The HIPAA issues are complex in foreign countries as some countries do not have such laws. However, enforcing an equivalent American patient privacy law in a destination hospital will contribute to a positive experience for all American medical tourists. Over the years, some popular medical tourism destination countries began to pass similar privacy laws. Malaysia and Mexico passed their version of the Personal Data Protection Act—an equivalent of healthcare privacy law in 2010. Singapore passed a similar act in 2014, and the law was updated in 2023. Both Thailand and India passed similar privacy laws in 2022 and 2023. HIPAA violation issues can become more complex in a cross-cultural setting. For instance, a technician or salesperson in the doctor's exam or operating room without the patients' consent can violate HIPAA. Nurses gossiping about a patient's condition in the hospital's hallway is another violation of HIPAA, even if it is done in a foreign language unspoken by the patient.

Legal Recourse

Medical negligence and malpractice are valid concerns for potential medical tourists. Every medical tourist should at least ask the question: How does one seek recourse if something goes wrong with my treatment? For the most part, nobody expects anything to go wrong if the hospitals are as good as they claim to be. Nevertheless, it is better to prepare oneself and know what to do if medical complications develop, potentially leading to litigation in medical negligence, medical malpractice, or both.

Which party is responsible for corporate negligence? The third-party payer, the facilitating company, or the foreign hospital? In the case of medical negligence, destination hospitals are more inclined to be responsible for hiring or retaining incompetent physicians negligently or for failing to supervise them adequately (Mirrer-Singer, 2007). In most cases, it is hard to prove corporate negligence by third-party payers or agents as they are not as directly involved. Fiduciary responsibilities can sometimes apply to third-party payers or facilitating agents in malpractice cases. In any case, any legal pursuit would likely apply the law of the destination country where the malpractice occurred. That country might not uphold the US corporate negligence law.

How should injured patients seek recourse abroad? Unfortunately, many destination countries are not legal-friendly regarding medical malpractice. Cortez (2012) concluded that there is no platform to adequately address or even resolve malpractice disputes in many of these destination countries—looking primarily at India or Thailand. The average payout in most destination countries is a small fraction of the US average malpractice claims. The patients would likely be dealing with an unfamiliar foreign language groping in a foreign legal system. They may even need to travel frequently to the destination country for court hearings and proceedings. It may be challenging for patients to obtain medical records or find a medical person to testify in court. Foreign legal systems can sometimes take up to twenty-five years to resolve a lawsuit, such as in India. In some countries like Mexico, there is an informal and less costly process of resolutions through an alternative government entity called Conamed (refer to Chapter 9) that may result in quicker but less compensation. Still, all these hassles make one question if it is even worth pursuing legal recourse. A recommended way to get around and prevent such issues is to purchase complications insurance for one's peace of mind right from the beginning, before the trip departure.

8

Issues Faced by Insurance Companies and Employers

Medical tourism's emergence has raised opportunities and impediments among third-party payers such as insurance companies or employers. On the one hand, if offshore treatments cost only a fraction of those in the United States, won't all third-party payers seize the opportunities, begin offering care abroad for their members, and save themselves tons of dollars? After all, several insurance companies, such as Blue Cross Blue Shield of South Carolina, Aetna, Anthem Wellpoint, and UnitedHealth Group, have already done so. Large employers such as Hannaford Brothers and HSM Solutions have followed suit. Why are there not more jumping on the bandwagon? The answer is more complex. In addition to what seems like a golden opportunity, there are impediments, concerns, and controversies faced by third-party payers regarding medical tourism. This chapter will address the motivations and impediments of third-party payers participating in this nascent market.

Adopters of Medical Tourism

Nearly every type of insurer, including Health Management Organizations (HMOs), Preferred Provider Organizations (PPOs), and self-insured employer plans, has explored the idea of medical tourism at some point. Some plans may provide members with financial incentives to have high-cost surgeries outside the country. Third-party payers adopting medical tourism can be classified as proactive or passive adopters. Early adopters are considered proactive in endorsing the concepts of medical tourism and rolling out their extensive offshore plans. Examples of early adopters are Blue Cross Blue Shield of South Carolina, Aetna, Anthem Wellpoint, and the UnitedHealth Group. They sought to cut costs by encouraging their members to receive medical tourism procedures abroad through cross-border plans (Medical Tourism Magazine, 2014). Companion Global Healthcare, Inc., a Blue Cross Blue Shield of South Carolina subsidiary, has embraced medical tourism strategies by contracting with hospitals in Costa Rica, Malaysia, Singapore, Thailand, and Turkey. On the other hand, passive adopters accept the idea of medical tourism without actively advertising for offshore services or encouraging their members to seek care abroad. However, patients can find approved international hospitals, mostly JCI-accredited, among their list of network providers. A good example is Blue Cross Blue Shield of North Carolina.

In 1999, California legislation passed a bill allowing insurance companies from the state to reimburse authorized providers in Mexico. Since then, numerous existing health plans have made medical tourism feasible. For instance, the California Blue Shield provider network offers low-cost premiums, including traveling to accredited hospitals in Mexico (Meštrović, 2023). MediExcel, a cross-border HMO offering employers group medical coverage in the San Diego area, began to include 24/7 access to routine doctor visits among its networks in Mexicali and Tijuana (Medical Tourism Magazine, 2014).

Aetna offers a benefits package that gives full coverage for eligible members and their dependents for qualified preventative care, including immunizations and wellness exams received in Mexicali, Tecate, and Tijuana (Medical Tourism Magazine, 2014). In February of 2014, Aetna launched a new partnership with Mexico's largest health insurer to offer high-end plans to approximately 30,000 members to access its provider network in the United States and Mexico (Meštrović, 2023). The partnership initiated by Aetna comes naturally as many Mexican immigrants and naturalized citizens living in states such as California and Texas would cross the border to access healthcare services, taking advantage of lower treatment costs in Mexico and the common language spoken by the doctors.

In 2007, Aetna International recognized medical tourism as a major upcoming trend and initiated a trial program by collaborating with hospitals in Singapore for costly medical procedures. The grocery chain Hannaford Brothers, headquartered in Maine, New England, utilized Aetna to allow employees to travel to Singapore for hip and knee replacement surgeries (Medical Tourism Magazine, 2014). Other insurance companies began to roll out their cross-border health plans individually. WellPoint introduced a pilot program in 2008 in which its members could undergo medical procedures in India. UnitedHealth Group, based in Florida, provides exclusive deals for surgeries and other medical tourism services at hospitals in Thailand.

International Adopters outside the United States

In Canada, private insurance covers approximately 15 percent of total healthcare spending. An estimated thirty million private individual and group policies have extended health insurance covering Canadians while they travel abroad for care. Approximately 64,000 Canadians traveled abroad for elective treatments in 2016. In 2023, an estimated 1.8 percent of Canadian patients traveled abroad for elective treatment (Yang, 2024). Gynecological and orthopedic surgery were two of the most sought-after procedures.

British United Provident Association (BUPA), Britain's largest private health insurer, has contracts with Ruby Hospital in India (Meštrović, 2023). Mumbai-based Wockhardt Hospital is also on BUPA's emergency international network of participating hospitals. In the European Union (EU), agreements among member nations have been set up to facilitate cross-border health care. European insurers must reimburse certain treatment costs utilized in other EU countries. European travelers can use their home insurance in any EU country or any country in the European Economic Area if they possess their European health insurance card or appropriate documentation.

Australia has reciprocal healthcare agreements for medical treatment abroad with eleven countries. These countries are Belgium, Finland, Ireland, Italy, Malta, New Zealand, Norway, Slovenia, Sweden, the Netherlands, and the UK (Better Health Channel, 2024). However, they are mostly limited to emergency treatments. Like the US Medicare, Medicare Australia is unlikely to cover overseas medical treatment, and private health insurance may not cover it either. Nevertheless, some private Australian insurers have begun to enter the medical tourism market. Reciprocal healthcare agreements basically cover the cost of essential medical treatments for Australians traveling in those countries, and they do not replace private health insurance for overseas travel.

Opportunities: What Are Their Motivations?

The opportunities to enter the medical tourism market abound, so what motivates third-party payers to consider participating in this emerging market initially? Among the significant motivations are cost savings, higher demand for medical tourism, and assurance of quality of care. In a survey gauging insurance companies' interest in medical tourism, out of a total of thirty-six respondents, the adopters of medical tourism (39 percent) cited cost cutting as the most crucial motivation to engage in the practice (Gan & Frederick, 2013b). They additionally cited a list of assurance of quality-of-care factors, such as hospital reputations, treatment outcomes, doctors' credentials, and advanced medical technology, among the top selection criteria to include a foreign hospital in their provider network

Cost Savings

As stated in previous chapters, American medical tourists can typically save 50 percent to 80 percent by traveling abroad for care for most elective treatments. Most Americans who seek offshore care are uninsured or underinsured, in addition to those who seek cosmetic surgeries, which are usually not covered by insurance companies. When medical tourism emerged in the mid-2000s, uninsured US persons rose from forty-six million in 2007 to fifty-one million in 2009. During the same period, the US healthcare expenditure rose from 17.3 percent of GDP in 2007 to around 17.6 percent in 2009 (DeNavas-Walt, Proctor, and Smith, 2010; Deloitte, 2011). The rising number of uninsured persons in the United States and the continued rise of healthcare expenditures have some third-party payers scrambling for solutions. They began looking into medical tourism as a feasible option for their members. Employers facing challenges in maintaining health coverage for their employees are trying self-funding with medical tourism to keep costs down.

Medical tourism is becoming an increasingly popular option for many self-insured employers struggling with the high cost of health care in the United States. HSM Solutions, a furniture manufacturer located in Hickory, NC, proposed to eliminate copays and deductibles, provide travel expenses for the employee and a companion, and offer a bonus equivalent to 20 percent of the company's savings, capped at $20,000 (Wojcik, 2013). When the idea of medical tourism was introduced to the 2,500 employees in fifty locations of HSM in 2007, many hesitated. Since then, 250 employees and dependents have taken advantage of the benefit of using offshore health care. HSM was estimated to save $9.5 million in healthcare costs over the first six years of implementing the new plan, and the savings began to accrue in the company's workers' compensation program (Wojcik, 2013). Due to the success of the medical tourism benefit plan, HSM has expanded the plan to include bariatric surgery, knee and hip replacement, and hernia operations.

The vast treatment cost differentials (even after factoring in travel costs) between the United States and the destination countries are essentially one of the pull factors that draw potential patients to medical tourism. Therefore, third-party payers would want to endorse medical tourism because more significant cost savings would bring in higher profits for them. But would they?

Demand for Medical Tourism

One of the concerning trends that will guarantee the growth of the medical tourism industry is the aging population in developed economies today or the coming of age of baby boomers. Baby boomers are defined as those who were born between 1946 and 1964. According to the Census Bureau, there are 76.4 million baby boomers in the United States in 2024. As of 2024, their age ranges from fifty-nine to seventy-seven. The estimated number of baby boomers in the United States, Canada, Europe, Australia, and New Zealand is around 220 million. They represent a sizable market for low-cost and high-quality medical, dental, and bariatric care.

A higher demand for medical tourism in the mid-2000s was one of the vital reasons for third-party payers to consider participating in medical tourism. In a survey conducted in 2008 to assess consumer interest in medical tourism, Deloitte found that 39 percent of respondents were open to undergoing an elective procedure in a foreign country. Additionally, 27 percent of participants indicated their willingness to seek treatment outside the United States, while 3 percent had already pursued medical care abroad (Deloitte, 2008). Deloitte reported that 750,000 Americans traveled for care outside the United States in 2007. The number was estimated to increase to 878,000 in 2010 and 1.3 million in 2011 (Deloitte, 2009; Deloitte, 2011). At that time, Deloitte forecasted that the number of American medical tourists would be five times higher in ten years.

Other push factors discussed in earlier chapters also play crucial roles in convicting some third-party payers to join the medical tourism bandwagon. These include more competition as an increasing number of US third-party players begin to offer international health plans and a growing number of facilitating firms to consult and work with.

Assurance of Quality of Care

Like the potential medical tourists, the potential third-party payers must convince themselves that lower costs do not necessarily mean lower quality of care. Quality of care refers to quality assurance, control procedures, clinical practice, and facility operation. A World Bank study on healthcare quality in developing economies indicated that it exceeds the minimum required standards in industrial economies (Mattoo & Rathindran, 2006). Escorts Heart Institute in India performed nearly 15,000 cardiac surgeries annually, with only a 0.8 percent mortality rate, which is 50 percent less than those reported by most major US hospitals (Hutchinson, 2005).

Moreover, the rapid development of US-affiliated international hospitals and medical education outside the United States has contributed to both the quality of foreign hospitals and the credentials of their physicians. Harvard Medical International has partnered with hospitals in over thirty countries; meanwhile, the Cleveland Clinic runs hospitals in Austria and Canada (Cohen, 2010). In Singapore, a prominent hospital is an extension of the esteemed Johns Hopkins University. Duke University received over $350 million from the Singapore government to create a graduate medical school with the National University of Singapore. Cornell University's Weill Cornell Medical College runs a medical school in Qatar (Turner, 2007). All these affiliations with reputable US medical centers and medical schools should convince the US third-party payers that the overall quality of the hospitals and professional standard of their physicians in many of these destination countries are above the international standard.

Furthermore, hospitals in destination countries that target patients from developed countries, such as the United States, often attempt to meet their expectations by advertising the number of physicians trained in US medical schools. For instance, the Bumrungrad Hospital in Thailand has many physicians and nurses with international experience. In addition to having at least 200 physicians being US board-certified, many of their doctors also have board certification from the UK, Australia, Germany, or Japan. Moreover, in many international hospitals, physicians are assisted by more registered nurses per patient than in similar facilities in developed economies. Some even offer single-patient rooms with a dedicated nurse 24/7. The third-party payers must agree that such services are unparalleled in any US hospital.

In addition, many of these foreign hospitals come equipped with international healthcare accreditations. Since the Joint Commission International (JCI) was established in 1999, over 120 hospitals and healthcare facilities in Asia, India, Europe, the Middle East, South America, and the Caribbean have received accreditation by 2007. By 2007, Singapore (eleven hospitals) and India (six hospitals) had received the most significant number of JCI-accredited hospitals in Asia. As of June 2024, there are 47 hospitals in India, 50 in Thailand, and 108 in the United Arab Emirates that are JCI-accredited. The accreditations should again assure the third-party payers of sending their members to accredited hospitals with high-quality healthcare services.

Advanced medical technology is another pull factor when considering the quality of an offshore hospital. Generally, the more updated the medical technology, the better the quality of care in the hospital. Many foreign hospitals mainly focus on advanced medical equipment and surgeries in their promotional efforts. For instance, Apollo Gleneagles Hospital in India promotes its PET or CT scan devices. A hospital in Thailand is promoting its Gamma Knife device, which is used for advanced and precise brain surgery. Acibadem Hospital in Turkey promotes the highest number of DaVinci robots. Additionally, there are alternative advanced medical procedures offered in countries other than the United States. For example, Thailand provides gender reassignment surgery, India offers less intrusive knee-resurfacing treatments, and Singapore is known for tooth-in-eye surgery. The US third-party payers should be aware that the overall standard of medical technology and surgeries performed in many of these foreign hospitals are on par or even a notch up than those of the US hospitals.

Impediments: What Are Their Concerns?

Despite all the favorable and timely push and pull factors pointing toward a positive environment in which to engage in the medical tourism business, most third-party payers in the United States still lag in offering offshore health plans. In the same survey cited earlier with insurance companies, non-adopters of medical tourism (61 percent) cited barriers that prevent them from providing medical tourism were "the assurance of patient safety in the foreign hospital" (90 percent), followed by "convincing domestic employers to cover treatment abroad" (84 percent) and "coordinating pre-care and post care with hospitals in the domestic country" (84 percent) (Gan & Frederick, 2013b). The following sections explain why US third-party payers are slow in endorsing medical tourism.

Perceived Lower Demand

The passing of the Affordable Care Act or Obamacare plans in 2010 reduced the number of uninsured in the United States. US uninsured persons declined from 46 million in 2007 to 25.3 million during 2020–3 (DeNavas-Walt, Proctor, and Smith, 2010; Tsai, 2023). During the same period, the US healthcare expenditure has risen from 17.3 percent of GDP in 2007 to 18 percent in 2023. As the healthcare cost continues to increase and almost half reduced the number of uninsured in recent years, the third-party payers may not see as urgent a need to participate in medical tourism as in the mid-2000s, that is, before the Obamacare plans came into effect in 2010.

On the other hand, some argue that due to the Affordable Care Act, millions of new uninsured people who need healthcare services are entering the healthcare system. Still, those people are likely to choose something at home other than medical tourism as an option, thus creating a sudden demand and supply shortage in the home healthcare system. Those who are likely to opt for offshore care are those who have been insured and now see longer wait times for surgeries, especially invasive ones.

Other Cost Concerns

For one, cost saving could be misleading. Some point out that the emphasis should be on the overall saving instead of just the saving from the treatment cost. Given the additional travel distance and unknown risks, it is said that only high treatment costs exceeding $25,000 in the United States are worth considering in any offshore health plans (Marlowe & Sullivan, 2007). In another estimate, some pointed out that "to ensure significant savings excluding travel expenses and patients' safety, such offshore care must be restricted to non-urgent, short-duration treatments costing more than $15,000 to $20,000 in the United States for conditions not aggravated by air travel." (Milstein & Smith, 2006). Indeed, third-party payers must remember that savings may be dampened by other expenditures such as airfares, accommodation, and meals for patients and a companion, financial incentives for the patients, possible vendor fees, and other administrative costs.

Another consideration for the employers is prolonged absenteeism from work by the patients, assuming additional pretesting before the surgery and post-surgery recuperation period before patients are fit to travel home. This consideration is especially crucial for employees residing in a state without government subsidies for offshore travel. Moreover, third-party payers face the complexity of dealing with an international billing system, which can include converting foreign exchanges and learning a different measurement standard, such as the metric system. To design a unique yet attractive plan, third-party payers may wish to outsource expertise such as legal service, risk management, software solutions, or partnering with an established facilitator. They may also need to consider investing in an additional department with extra managers, customer service employees, and lawyers. Other hidden risk costs are to be considered, including expenses related to patient safety and travel risk and costs involved in international legal recourse if things go wrong.

Patient Safety

From third-party payers' viewpoint, cost savings are not the only factor they are considering. More importantly, they are concerned about the patient's safety, especially health outcomes and travel risk, and their responsibilities if something goes wrong. After all, medical tourists will likely face potential risks that may compromise their safety as they travel to another country to seek care throughout their journey.

For starters, there may be a need for more communication and discussion between foreign doctors and patients before the surgery concerning whether the procedure is necessary. Third-party payers may want to review the foreign doctor's notes to justify certain procedures and for any pre-authorization purposes. The doctor's notes benefit the insurance companies, given that most foreign hospitals do not use the same US medical procedure codes heavily relied on by US insurance companies for billing purposes.

Moreover, like most other countries, the United States does not require hospitals to measure and report surgical outcomes or participate in international performance-measurement systems. Therefore, comparing relative quality is difficult (Milstein & Smith, 2006). For instance, one may interpret a report such as "Apollo Hospital chain has maintained a 99 percent success rate in more than 50,000 cardiac surgeries performed" as a signal of quality of care. Cohen (2010) emphasized that "mortality rates are a simplistic indicator of quality" and may not capture the issues that could arise during postoperative recovery. Post-care is one of the most critical aspects of patient safety. However, it can be challenging for third-party payers to deal with because it may be hindered by a lack of medical records regarding the procedure performed outside the country, and patients may face the risk of infection. For instance, they may be exposed to antibiotic-resistant bacteria that can cause complications after surgery. In 2004, the Centers for Disease Control and Prevention (CDC) reported twelve cases of US females developing nontuberculous mycobacterial infections from cosmetic surgery in the Dominican Republic (Centers for Disease Control and Prevention, 2004). In 2023, the center again reported ten cases of fungal meningitis from epidural anesthesia among US persons who traveled to two cosmetic clinics in Mexico.

Eight patients died (Centers for Disease Control and Prevention, 2023). The third-party payers would want to advise their members to check with the CDC websites before traveling to a particular country for care.

Furthermore, there may be a need for patients to follow up after the surgery to ensure the outcomes are satisfactory and safe, as they may require additional treatment after returning to the United States, which the insurance may not cover. The third-party payers would want to communicate the specific coverage clearly to their members before their departure. There are potential financial risks due to limited coverage by travel insurance. Suppose complications develop during or after the procedure. In that case, patients may not be covered by their medical or travel insurance. They could face significant emergency evacuation costs to their home countries if there are complications. The third-party payers may advise their members to take up more comprehensive travel insurance that covers medical evacuation or a separate "health travel insurance" that covers medical complications (e.g., one that is sold by Medical Tourism Corporation, mentioned in Chapter 7), or complications insurance sold by a few other agencies mentioned in Chapter 5.

In the case of post-surgery complications, a lack of continuity of care may require patients to seek a different doctor in the United States to fix the problem. However, some US doctors may be unwilling to assume medical responsibility for patients who undergo procedures outside the county (Marlowe & Sullivan, 2007). Some of their reasons are that they are unaware of the quality of work that has been performed overseas, the unavailability of medical records, and the possibility of dealing with an impending malpractice suit. However, despite the ethical dilemma of treating patients without being involved in their surgeries, some doctors, such as those from the American Board of Plastic Surgeons (ABPS), decided to abide by the ethical code by prioritizing patient safety and are willing to deliver prompt care to help those who had undergone botched cosmetic surgeries outside the country (Iorio et al., 2014).

Moreover, post-surgery complications may eventually lead to malpractice suits, which, unfortunately, are plagued by poor regulatory systems in some destination countries, as pointed out in Chapter 9. A case in point is Joshua Goldberg, a 23-year-old American, who died from a mysterious heart failure while receiving care in Bumrungrad International Hospital in 2006. The hospital became the target of a criminal investigation and lawsuit. While medical accidents can happen in any hospital worldwide, even a good one, such a report raises troubling questions among third-party payers. Moreover, despite best efforts to work with only "quality" hospitals, there will always be a risk of surgical complications that could develop into a public relations nightmare. Poor quality of medical care not only creates additional medical costs, travel costs, and legal costs for both patients and the third-party payers, but they can also reflect poorly on the credibility of the third-party payers (Yang, 2011). Third-party players would undoubtedly want to weigh all their pros and cons carefully before participating in medical tourism.

Travel Risks

Travel risk is usually closely related to the specific destination country for which the patient travels for care. Medical tourists may face potential medical risks when traveling on long international flights. They may be exposed to new germs and bacteria, making them vulnerable to certain disease infections (York, 2008). The low oxygen level in an airplane on a long flight can prove challenging for those with lung conditions (Forgione & Smith, 2006). Patients undergoing cardiac surgery may be more susceptible to deep vein thrombosis during the flight. Further, there are risks around the fitness to fly—traveling too soon after a medical procedure is risky. Foreign doctors are responsible for ensuring their patients have enough recovery time before they are fit to fly.

The socioeconomic condition of a destination country is also a part of travel risk. In some developing countries, hospital employees (e.g., nurses, cooks, and janitors) may not be highly aware of sanitation; patients are, therefore, more likely to contract a severe disease infection from the hospital (Forgione & Smith, 2006). For instance, the rate of incidents of infectious diseases such as HIV is much higher in some countries, such as South Africa, than in the United States.

The environmental condition of the destination country may also adversely affect the outcomes of patients' procedures. For instance, the hot and sunny tropical climate may expose medical tourists to a rapid change in temperature and humility, which can impact their health outcomes in terms of prolonged hospital stay and complication rate, especially among elderly surgical patients (Gautam, Kathuria, and Chhabra, 2011).

The cultural condition of a country also matters. Suppose most individuals at the destination do not communicate in English or do not have a rudimentary language understanding. In that case, patients are at a higher risk of experiencing emotions such as loneliness, isolation, anxiety, and vulnerability due to the lack of effective communication (Hery et al., 2023). This could hurt their recovery and overall state of being. There are additional concerns, such as the stress involved in having treatments in a foreign country, away from the support of friends and family.

Because these travel-related and country-specific risks affect patient safety and treatment outcomes, they are essential factors for third-party payers to consider before participating in medical tourism. After all, the fiduciary duty of third-party sponsors is to provide their members with competitive, transparent, and ethical health offerings that help them access high-quality medical care at a cost-effective rate.

Legal Liabilities

Two major questions arise if third-party payers actively participate in medical tourism and promote its activities. The first is, "Is it legal for insurers or employers to ask their members to leave the country for care?" The second is, "What is the fiduciary responsibility of a third-party payer in case of malpractice?"

Currently, no law prevents international medical travel. The American Medical Association (AMA), American College of Surgeons (ACS), and American Dental Association (ADA) have all issued statements recognizing patients' rights to choose their physicians and hospitals. They all highlight the importance of post-care and their related financial responsibilities. ACS specifically supports the view that third-party payers should be responsible for coordinating and reimbursing post-care in the United States, including managing complications, readmission, rehabilitation, and long-term care.

Suppose something goes wrong with a medical procedure, and patients want to sue. In that case, self-funded insurers have barely any liability for getting sued for medical malpractice because ERISA governs the suits in federal courts (Galentine, 2013). Even in gross negligence claims against doctors, the courts usually will not find the employers liable. However, the process is entirely different for fully insured insurers. The facilitators and employers are likely liable because the jurisdiction for such cases is in state court. Therefore, self-funded employers must carefully choose which medical tourism facilitating companies to work with, paying close attention to referring hospitals, doctors, and the trip planner. Some hospitals do not meet HIPAA privacy requirements, exposing employers to potential liability. By contracting with reputable hospitals, self-funded employers allow the hospitals to take on the liability issues.

Politically, Is It Correct?

Undoubtedly, some insurers are more adventurous and willing to develop creative plans. However, others use the plans as leverage to negotiate lower prices with domestic healthcare providers. Since medical insurance has traditionally been considered non-portable, care outside the county is only covered if, in the case of an emergency, portable insurance plans hardly rouse the interest of federal or state laws that govern medical insurance (Cortez, 2012). A good example is federally funded insurance such as Medicare, which only covers emergency care outside the United States. Moreover, it may not be politically popular to use public funds to pay for offshore healthcare providers who are direct competitors to the US providers.

On the state level, at least two states have considered bills that would encourage state public employees to travel outside the country for surgery. The first is a well-publicized bill that died in the West Virginia legislature. In West Virginia, two house bills that favor medical tourism were submitted to the state legislature in 2006. Under House Bill 4359, state employees could travel outside the country for surgery at JCI-accredited hospitals. The benefits would cover all treatment costs, a waiver of all copayments and deductibles, air tickets, and lodging for the employee and a companion. The employee would also receive a rebate of 20 percent of the cost savings. The second bill (House Bill 4711) is like the first bill, except it sets up a system for private insurance companies to participate. In 2007, a similar proposal was also attempted by the Colorado legislature. Unfortunately, it was not being considered earnestly.

Private insurers in the United States have made more progress than public insurers regarding medical tourism, as shown from examples of early adopters given earlier in the chapter. California and Texas have laws that address private plans related to medical tourism. Texas forbids HMOs and other state-regulated insurers from requiring beneficiaries to go abroad or offering financial incentives to induce them to do so (Cortez, 2012). On the other hand, California permits plans that contract with providers in Mexico, subject to various requirements, as mentioned earlier in the chapter.

Insurance plans offered under the Employee Retirement Income Security Act (ERISA) are one type of insurance protected from state regulations, thus giving them more room to explore the option to include medical tourism. These are often self-funded plans that larger employers or industrial or professional organizations offer. One example is offering self-funded ERISA plans by the

Western Growers Association (WGA) to immigrant agricultural workers in California and the Southwest region (Cortez, 2012). Under the plan, the recipients can add "riders" to their plans to seek care in Mexico. The WGA develops various plans by contracting and working with primary care and specialty providers in Mexico and the United States. However, if medical tourism plans become more noticeable, domestic providers can unite to ban such plans, as they did in Texas.

Moreover, employers may face opposition from unions for participation in medical tourism, as in the classic case of Blue Ridge Paper, Inc. in North Carolina. To save potential costs of $80,000 for treatment in the United States, the company offered to pay for treatment and airfares expenses plus $10,000 cash to one of its union employees to travel to India for gallbladder removal and rotator cuff surgeries (McLean, 2007). The union filed suit, went public with its opposition, and forced the company to abandon its plan.

What began as innovative offshore health plans by employers can end up with active opposition by the unions. The labor unions are worried that when employees seek medical treatment overseas, it might be seen as a form of outsourcing. This could lead to legal consequences and the risk of job cuts in the American healthcare sector. (Meštrović, 2023). On the other hand, for successful employers such as HSM Solutions, if their employees know they can save out-of-pocket expenses and get a bonus, it puts both the employers and employees in a partnership. Cost savings can be reinvested into the company's healthcare expenditures to further expand offshore health service offerings and benefit more employees. Not only does this help to engender trust between employees and employers, but it also demonstrates a forward-thinking corporate culture. It is a win-win situation.

Even with deep cost savings, international accreditations of foreign hospitals, assurance of patient safety and travel risks, and low risk of liability, there can never be 100 percent guarantee, so there is a certain percentage of risk to engage in medical tourism on the part of third-party sponsors. There is currently no federal regulation on medical insurance that covers medical tourism. All these may explain why so many insurance companies are still hesitant to participate in medical tourism despite some favorable factors. Like all other businesses, third-party payers must be willing to take risks to stay competitive. They may conduct due diligence research and hospital visits, then negotiate and contract with reputable hospitals directly without using an intermediary. They can start with a few treatments with a few US-affiliated hospitals, then slowly expand the coverage of procedures and hospitals over time.

9

Regulatory and Ethical Issues

This chapter will introduce deeper regulatory and ethical issues surrounding seeking treatment in another state or country. We will examine how these international or interstate issues have impacted health safety. Examples of interstate treatments are abortion, in vitro fertilization (IVF), and the use of cannabis for medicinal purposes. Examples of international treatments are many, including controversial ones such as IVF, stem cell therapy, and organ transplantations. International legal and ethical issues surrounding stem cell therapy, organ transplantations, and reproductive tourism, to a lesser extent, have already been discussed in Chapter 2. In this chapter, in addition to regulatory and ethical issues faced by international medical tourists, we will focus mainly on interstate issues concerning abortion, IVF, and the use of medical cannabis.

International Issues and Impacts on Health Safety: General Treatments

First, regulatory issues affecting typical medical tourists who seek popular treatments abroad will be discussed before diving into complex issues faced by those seeking more controversial treatments. Among the regulatory issues confronting international medical tourists are HIPAA compliance by foreign hospitals, medical malpractice, corporate negligence, and the fiduciary responsibility of insurers or employers. Ethical issues evolve mainly around the foreign physician–patient relationship, especially when medical complications arise.

First, we will examine medical tourism's regulatory ambiguities by addressing some interesting legal questions. For instance, is it illegal for residents to leave their state or country for health care, especially one involving procedures not approved in the home state or country? Do all host countries have HIPAA-compliant laws similar to the United States? Can US patients sue providers outside the country for malpractice? What about the corporate negligence of foreign hospitals or facilitators? Equally important are insurance-related questions. Is it legal for insurers or employers to ask patients to seek care abroad? What is the fiduciary responsibility of the insurers or employers in case of medical complications? Since the last two questions have been addressed in Chapter 8, we will omit them in this chapter.

Can They Leave the Country?

Current federal and state laws do not explicitly allow or disallow US patients from leaving the country for medical care. After all, many celebrities and US presidents have done it for decades. Furthermore, whether a particular trip is illegal depends on the motivation behind the trip, the destination country, and the treatment. Indeed, patients have various motivations to seek care outside their home countries. It may be to seek treatments that are not accessible, banned by law, not offered by domestic healthcare providers, or not paid by insurance companies. For instance, women from predominantly Catholic countries travel to more permissible jurisdictions for abortion. A good example is Polish women who began traveling to England, Germany, Belgium, Spain, and the Czech Republic to access legal abortions since the total abortion ban was implemented in Poland in 2020.

Another example is US cancer patients traveling to clinics in Mexico for laetrile, a drug that the FDA has not approved. However, another example is US patients traveling to Europe or Asia for a new hip resurfacing technology that the FDA delayed approving. The damaged bone is scraped away in this procedure and replaced with chrome alloy. The procedure costs less, and it causes less postoperative trauma than the conventional replacement procedure done in the United States. However, motivations to travel can become more complex and unclear regarding controversial treatments banned in the United States. These will be discussed later in the chapter.

HIPAA Compliance

The Health Insurance Portability and Accountability Act (HIPAA) of 1996 is a significant health privacy law within the US healthcare system. This law was set up to protect patients' information and restrict how their health information may be used or shared. A violation of HIPAA can result in civil penalties of $100 per noncompliance, capped at an annual maximum of $25,000. It can also bring about criminal charges against anyone who knowingly obtains or discloses individually identifiable health information, which violates HIPAA (Forgione & Smith, 2006).

The stringent HIPAA laws apply in the United States, and US medical insurance plans must follow these rules, even for service providers outside the country. However, except for Europe, most destination countries outside the United States do not have HIPAA or its equivalents. Asia is considered more relaxed in terms of patient privacy. When considering medical tourism, American patients must consider such policy issues, which can present potential risks of traveling abroad for care. The US medical tourism facilitators can address these privacy issues by including HIPAA standards in their contracts with foreign healthcare providers (Forgione & Smith, 2006).

Medical Malpractice

Can injured US patients seek recourse overseas? For good reasons, the medical tourism market prefers patients to resolve disputes outside the United States. Many destination countries are notoriously unfriendly when it comes to medical malpractice. While the average compensation for medical malpractice claims in the United States is around $330,000, the average payout for Thailand and Mexico is only $3,000 and $4,800, respectively (Cortez, 2012). Moreover, medical tourists may have to deal with an unfamiliar foreign language when navigating a foreign legal system. They may also need to make multiple trips to the destination country for court hearings and proceedings. Foreign court rulings may not be as efficient as in the United States. For instance, it can take up to fifteen–twenty-five years to resolve a lawsuit in India! One reason is medical tourists are not allowed to file their cases in Indian courts; instead, their only recourse is through State and National Consumer Disputes Redressal Commissions, which have a huge backlog (Chinai & Goswami, 2007).

Foreign healthcare providers are not particularly cooperative either, often refusing to furnish patients with copies of their medical records. It can be challenging for patients to prove what exactly happened. Further, finding a foreign medical professional willing to testify on the patient's behalf is challenging. In many destination countries, there is a general reluctance to challenge medical authority, and patients are often discouraged from filing valid complaints (Cortez, 2012). In a nutshell, most destination countries lack a platform to address or resolve malpractice disagreements.

It is worth pointing out that the Mexican government set up an independent agency called Comision National de Arbitraje Medico (Conamed) in 1996 to handle malpractice cases through conciliation and arbitration. Since then, this informal and less costly channel has resolved two-thirds of malpractice cases outside the courts. The alternative process hastens the conflict resolution, and the arbiter is generally more knowledgeable in medical issues than a lawyer (Tena-Tamayo & Sotelo, 2005). Arbitration usually takes three to six months for conciliation and fifteen months for sentencing. Agreements are reached without referring to the legal authority. The total amount awarded is usually less than that awarded by a court since lawyer fees and court costs are avoided (Tena-Tamayo & Sotelo, 2005). Most patients and doctors who have used the service have been satisfied.

Corporate Negligence

It is essential to understand that medical tourism facilitating firms are legally responsible for the torts they commit, including corporate negligence. Under the corporate negligence theory, hospitals can be held accountable for negligently hiring or retaining incompetent physicians or failing to supervise them adequately (Mirrer-Singer, 2007). However, this theory may not be applied consistently to insurance companies or facilitating firms. Due to additional obstacles, patients may encounter more challenges when suing an insurance company. For example, some states have granted HMOs immunity from negligent treatment suits (Bobinski, Hall, & Orentlicher, 2007). Additionally, a court hearing would likely apply the law of the country where the alleged malpractice occurred. That country might not recognize the US corporate negligence theory.

Potential medical tourists should know that proving corporate negligence is complex and challenging. It requires patients to establish the doctor's incompetence, the facilitating firm's knowledge of this incompetence, and a pattern of misconduct by the doctor (Mirrer-Singer, 2007). Proving negligent supervision is equally challenging, as it necessitates demonstrating that adequate supervision could have prevented the doctor's negligence or that prompt action post-incident could have minimized injuries. Moreover, it is challenging to establish that increased oversight by the medical tourism firm could have averted the doctor's negligence.

International Healthcare Law

Various countries' healthcare laws govern their respective hospital website marketing. Laws restrict multiple countries regarding what type of health information they can advertise on their websites. For instance, Turkish hospitals are not allowed to publish treatment prices and success outcomes on their websites (Inci, 2012), unlike hospitals in Singapore. The lack of easily obtained treatment success and pricing information may influence consumers' decision to go to Singapore instead of Turkey. The Jordanian and Korean hospitals have only begun to permit telemedicine during the Covid-19 pandemic in 2020 (Jin, 2021). The unavailability of telemedicine using the convenience of internet technologies such as Zoom may affect post-care follow-ups, prompting the patients to spend more money and effort to make another physical visit to the country. This, again, may affect the consumer's decision to choose a particular destination country over another.

Interstate Issues and Impacts on Health Safety in the United States

In this section, we will discuss interstate regulatory and ethical issues concerning abortion, IVF, and the use of medical cannabis. We will look at how these issues may directly impact the health safety of these procedures and products and indirectly affect the health safety of other procedures or services.

Abortion

As mentioned in Chapter 6, the US Supreme Court's landmark ruling in overturning *Roe v. Wade* in June 2022 has ended the constitutional right to abortion federally. The discretion on the legality of abortion has now passed to the individual states. At least fourteen states have a total abortion ban, and more states are following suit. The new ruling has sparked a new chapter of debates between the two opposite viewers.

Moral Issues

The debate surrounding abortion is primarily concerned with the moral status of the embryo and the fetus. If the fetus is regarded as a person with a life equivalent to that of any human being, then few would argue that abortion is justifiable. This is because it is not morally acceptable to kill children on the grounds of their illegitimacy, undesirability, or disability (Steinbock, 2024). Even if one agrees that the fetus is a person, it does not necessarily mean that it has the right to use the body of the woman who is pregnant. The morality of abortion is, therefore, dependent not only on the fetus's personhood but also on the pregnant woman's bodily autonomy.

There is a lot of controversy and strong emotions surrounding abortion in American politics. In terms of the morality of abortion, Americans are closely split; in 2020, a slight majority (47 percent) believed it to be morally wrong, while 44 percent thought it to be morally acceptable (Gallup, 2023a). However, this trend was reversed in 2023, with only 41 percent considering it morally wrong and 52 percent believing it morally acceptable (Gallup, 2023b). The Gallup poll also provided similar figures on the order of moral acceptability of other issues, with birth control being the most acceptable (88 percent), followed by smoking marijuana (70 percent), having a baby outside of marriage (70 percent), gambling (69 percent), gay or lesbian relationships (64 percent), stem cell research using human embryos (63 percent), doctor-assisted suicide (53 percent), sex between teenagers (43 percent), pornography (39 percent), and suicide (20 percent) (Gallup, 2023b). It is interesting to see that abortion (52 percent) is deemed more acceptable than sex between teenagers (43 percent) but less acceptable than having a baby outside of marriage (70 percent) or stem cell research using human embryos (63 percent).

Regulatory Issues

Nebraska prohibited all abortions after twenty weeks in 2010, stating that the fetus can feel pain at that stage. Over sixteen states followed suit with similar laws. In 2015, the House of Representatives passed the Pain-Capable Unborn Child Protection Act. However, the Senate withdrew the motion to consider the bill. The act restricted doctors from performing abortions after twenty weeks, except when necessary to save the life of a pregnant woman or in cases of rape or incest against a minor. In 2016, Utah became the first state to mandate that women having an abortion at twenty weeks or later must receive anesthesia. However, Texas passed one of the most stringent laws in 2021 that outlaws abortion after detecting a fetal heartbeat, usually after six weeks of pregnancy. In 2022, Oklahoma passed a law prohibiting abortion and categorized it as a felony offense, which can lead to imprisonment of up to ten years. At the same time, Louisiana proposed House Bill 813, which permits prosecuting those who undergo or perform abortions with murder charges. Later, a revised version of HB 813 was passed by the House, eliminating the language about charging women having abortions with murder and exempting birth control from being outlawed.

Interstate abortion laws that have been passed since the overturning of *Roe v. Wade* in June 2022 may have implications for health safety. As of November 2023, fourteen states have prohibited most abortions, while twenty-one states have protected them (KFF, 2023). Providers and supporters of abortion in many states have challenged the ban, citing violations of state constitutions or other state laws. Legal cases have tackled issues such as the availability of medication abortion and whether states can prevent their residents from crossing state lines to access abortion.

All state anti-abortion laws currently include a provision for "medical emergency" as an exception. However, there has been much uncertainty surrounding the definition of a medical emergency. For example, will a doctor perform an abortion on a pregnant woman who has a health condition that may or may not be life-threatening? In Texas, several women have brought a lawsuit alleging that they were denied medically necessary abortions (Steinbock, 2024). They, along with a few physicians, are seeking a clear answer as to when abortions are allowed under state law.

The *Dobbs v. Jackson* (popularly known as the "*Dobbs* decision" that led to the Supreme Court's overturning *Roe v. Wade*), which restricts access to abortion in Mississippi, has raised concerns about the impact it may have on pregnant patients' care. According to Steinbock (2024), the decision is likely to make it harder for physicians to treat their pregnant patients properly, especially those with chronic conditions like diabetes and heart disease. This could lead to increased burdens and complications for pregnant women who need abortions for medical reasons. The decision also raises questions about how close to death a woman must be for physicians to act and whether doctors will be willing to take risks and face possible jail time if their decisions are later questioned.

Eleven states do not permit exceptions for pregnancy resulting from rape or incest. The argument against such exceptions is that it is not right to end a pregnancy simply because the father was the result of rape. Conversely, those who are in favor of such exceptions believe it is unjust to compel women to carry a pregnancy that they did not choose.

Spillover Effects on Other Health Safety Issues

In light of the *Dobbs* decision, other reproductive services, such as IVF, may face negative consequences. This is because it is common practice to discard embryos, which could be impacted by the ruling. Typically, multiple embryos are created during IVF to allow doctors to implant two or fewer embryos per cycle while freezing the remaining embryos in the lab for future use. Additionally, testing embryos for defects and discarding the defective ones is also a routine practice in IVF. This is because the chances of defective embryos successfully implanting are low, and the chances of them miscarrying are high. By testing them, the likelihood of a successful pregnancy increases.

In February of 2024, the Supreme Court of Alabama held that frozen embryos are children concerning Alabama's wrongful death statutes. As a result, there has been concern that this may lead to a potential ban on the discarding of embryos in the state's IVF facilities (Sharfstein, 2024). Because the implications of the court's decision are unclear, IVF providers and patients are left with uncertainty. As a result, the University of Alabama's health system has decided to pause its IVF treatments while considering the consequences of the court's decision. In the meantime, pro-life groups such as Students for Life Action have expressed their intention to target the regulation of IVF embryos in the future. They view the practice as "ending most lives conceived in a lab."

The *Dobbs* decision raises concern not only about IVF but also about miscarriage. In the event of a miscarriage, the fetus dies within the uterus but is not naturally expelled from the woman's body. Sometimes, not all fetal tissue is released, which can lead to infections and endanger the mother's life. To address this, doctors may either wait for the miscarriage to occur naturally, which can take a few weeks, or prescribe surgical or abortion medication to extract the fetus or fetal tissue. However, banning abortion could have severe consequences for these procedures, as doctors may not be willing to perform procedures that could be perceived as illegal abortions. Women who lost a desired pregnancy may have to wait for weeks, which could add to their emotional stress and, in some cases, even endanger their lives. In Texas, for example, a doctor had to wait until the fetal heartbeat stopped before intervening in a woman's miscarriage, which led to a life-threatening infection in her uterus (Tanner, 2022).

In Vitro Fertilization (IVF)

As of September 2023, only twenty-one states plus Washington, DC, have passed fertility insurance coverage law. Out of these twenty-two jurisdictions, only fifteen of those laws include IVF coverage, and seventeen of them cover fertility preservation for iatrogenic (or medically induced) infertility. There are some state limitations. For instance, California excludes IVF from the mandate. In contrast, Texas mandates that insurance companies notify employers about the coverage's existence. However, these companies are not obliged to offer the coverage, and employers are not compelled to incorporate it into their healthcare plans (Leonhardt, 2019).

Regulatory Issues

Regulatory issues can hinder patients' access to services in their home countries, leading them to travel abroad for necessary treatment. The reasons could be due to ineligibility for treatment based on factors such as sexual orientation, marital status, or age limit for publicly funded health care. Additionally, some patients may travel to ensure the anonymity of donors, which may not be possible in their home countries. Others may seek more options or information regarding donor selection, which may not be offered in their country of origin. Each country may have specific ethical or religious considerations that limit the accessibility of certain IVF technologies or procedures. For instance, third-party egg or sperm donations are not allowed in Turkey. However, different countries have varying restrictions on social gender selection or cryopreservation (the freezing) of embryos, with some prohibiting commercial surrogacy and commercial egg donation, such as most European countries, Australia, Canada, and Japan.

Health Safety

Without supporting physicians in patients' home countries, medical tourists who undertake international reproductive services are often on their own, especially concerning treatment protocols and discerning the quality of care provided by foreign clinics (Whittaker, 2012). Although the European Society for Human Reproduction and Embryology publishes a "good practice guide" for clinics treating international patients, that is an exception. Since treatment protocols, quality of care, and expectations vary from country to country, it pays for potential patients to conduct their research before embarking on the journey. Many of them contact offshore clinics through the Internet or medical tourism facilitators. As such, they may need help comparing standards of care among clinics and countries. Potential patients may only be fully informed about various medical risks with guidance from a referring physician. For instance, there may be differences concerning the types of drugs and how they are administered, the number of embryos transferred, whether cryopreservation (freezing of embryos) is allowed, and whether counseling or other types of social support are available when needed (Whittaker, 2012).

In many instances, the very reason that some procedures are available in specific countries is because of a lack of regulation that translates into less consumer protection. It is, therefore, wise for potential patients to get independent legal advice, especially if they intend to contract surrogacy services such as bringing a baby home, having a foreign surrogate travel to their country, or importing frozen embryos, eggs, or sperm from another country (Whittaker, 2012). Further, they should check with their insurance companies to see if they will cover any post-care complications upon returning home. These are all delicate issues that should be carefully considered before engaging in an offshore IVF service.

Ethical Issues

In the case of offshore IVF services, we know very little about the recruitment and experiences of potential egg donors or surrogates involved. There is also little knowledge regarding whether these individuals involved have received any screening or counseling, the number of times they have donated, or whether they are protected from risks such as lower future fertility because of surgical procedures they must undertake (Whittaker, 2012). One ethical concern is that the growing demand for IVF services is encouraging a market for these body products and services, resulting in the bodies and health of poorer women being exploited. Studies have shown that even in developed countries such as Europe, there is still a lack of transparency over the sources and circumstances under which human eggs are obtained. Even though commercial surrogacy is forbidden in many countries due to ethical concerns over the commodification of female bodies and reproduction, it is legal in some states in the United States. It is the only form of surrogacy allowed in India until 2017. In India, surrogate women tend to be poor and illiterate; some argue that if these women are fully informed and voluntarily consent to be surrogates. As pointed out, the most vulnerable surrogates and egg donors are those who travel offshore. "These situations can involve two or more countries with conflicting laws and jurisdictional requirements, making it very difficult to regulate or provide any legal protection to those involved" (Whittaker, 2012).

Another ethical consequence concerns the rights of children to know about their biological parents and the lack of any information in the case of international (or intranational) anonymous egg donation. The long-term consequence is that these children may never have access to information on their biological heritage. In the case of pop singer Michael Jackson's three children, unlike his two older siblings who can easily verify who their common sperm-donating biological father is, would BG, his third child, supposedly his only biological child, be deprived ethically and emotionally if he ever wishes to find out who his biological surrogate mother is? The answer is not known because the IVF regulations in some states and countries are structured in such a way that the identity of the surrogate mother is protected. The double-blind identity could be a win-win situation for both parents in such celebrity cases. For the mother, to protect her from being scrutinized by the media and the public inquiries; for the father, to avoid fighting legal custody later in life.

Gender Selection

Another controversial reproductive technology is the gender selection of a child using certain complex IVF technologies. Gender selection for social reasons is banned in many countries, such as Canada, the UK, Australia, Japan, and China. It is defined as gender discrimination under numerous international conventions. However, it is legal in Belgium, Finland, Greece, North Cyprus, India, Jordan, and most states that allow IVFs in the United States.

Gender selection generates mixed views, given its medical, ethical, and societal implications. The argument for it centers on patient autonomy and reproductive freedom. The argument against it revolves around the unknown risks of the procedures to the offspring, potential misuse of medical resources for nonmedical purposes (Lieman & Breborowicz, 2014), possible inciting of societal gender discrimination, and perpetuation of social injustice (Ethics Committee of the American Society for Reproductive Medicine, 2022). The slippery slope concern is also raised, that is, once the threshold of applying the technology for one nonessential procedure is crossed, it may lead to selecting other non-health related traits such as intelligence or physical appearance in embryos—which may be ethically problematic.

Furthermore, some argue that such elective gender selection may violate the ethical principle of justice as it may result in significant gender imbalances in society, which leads to concerns for social stability. One justice concern is that the practice may use resources otherwise available for the treatment of infertility. Further, since insurance will not cover these elective procedures, the expenses will have to be paid out-of-pocket; only patients of a particular economic class can afford them, which might not be equitable. Moreover, the concerns about the risk of gender bias and social injustice are significant, especially in countries such as China or India, where many girls are "missing" because of infanticide or abortion (Ethics Committee of the American Society for Reproductive Medicine, 2022).

A survey of public attitudes found that over 70 percent of Americans disapprove of elective gender selection for nonmedical reasons (Hudson, Scott, and Kalfoglou, 2002). A similar German study found that only 8 percent approved the practice for nonmedical reasons (Hershberger & Pierce, 2010). In the UK, it was reported that public opposition to gender selection superseded reproductive autonomy claims (Herissone-Kelly, 2006).

The movement of parents, reproductive cells, embryos, and surrogates across the globe is posing challenges for ethical and regulatory frameworks. To help parents make informed decisions, it is crucial to provide them with accurate information and improve transparency regarding the recruitment of donors and services. In terms of reproductive travel overseas, potential medical tourists must comprehend both the advantages and the bioethical dilemmas and risks involved.

Use of Medical Cannabis

In the United States, no one can deny that smoking marijuana for recreational purposes has been a controversial topic for decades. However, the controversies extend even to the use of cannabis for medicinal purposes. In the following section, we will limit our discussion to regulatory and ethical issues surrounding medical cannabis and their impact on health safety.

Regulatory Issues

Until the Marihuana Tax Act was passed in 1937, marijuana was prescribed commonly in the United States, which might be unexpected for some readers. The act prohibited the use of marijuana. The passage of the Controlled Substances Act by President Nixon in 1970 has effectively classified marijuana under Schedule I drugs along with heroin, LSD, and ecstasy, when, in fact, marijuana is in no way as dangerous as any of those named substances. Drugs under Schedule I are designated the most dangerous "with a high risk of addiction and no currently accepted medical treatment use." Because of this designation, there is only a limited number of licenses permitted by the Drug Enforcement Administration (DEA) to perform clinical research using marijuana. In addition, expensive and time-consuming clinical trials have been previously supported by pharmaceutical companies that want exclusive patent rights to their products.

Since medical marijuana is not under any patent protection, there is less incentive for pharmaceutical companies to fund the clinical trials (Sagy et al., 2018). Scientific research on the medical effects of marijuana has been further restricted by the fact that the National Institute of Health must publicly fund all studies. The DEA has rejected attempts to reassign marijuana to a Schedule II drug because "there was no scientific evidence showing that it was better than other approved drugs for any specific medical condition." The DEA also cited the fact that the FDA has not officially declared the use of marijuana as "being a safe and effective drug for any indications." The federal government's objection to the use of medical marijuana is based on a national policy of zero-tolerance toward illicit drugs. Moreover, since 1972, the US government has successfully obstructed the scientific communities from research on marijuana.

Because marijuana remains a Schedule I drug, there is no regulated pharmacy system for marijuana. Thus, there is no control over its purity or potency. When the federal government took action to close down the Cannabis Buyers Club in California, patients with real medical needs for the drug were forced to buy from the black market, which contains contaminants. One primary argument for proposing to shift the marijuana classification to Schedule II is so that it could be prescribed and obtained through controlled and regulated channels (Clark, 2000). However, the Federal government fears the change in classification may open the door to the slippery slope that could result in the legalization of marijuana and send the wrong message to children about condoning the use of illicit drugs.

Findings on Medical Cannabis

Many scientific and medical research have confirmed the benefits of using marijuana or cannabis to treat various medical conditions. The most notable ones include Alzheimer's, Crohn's disease, epilepsy, glaucoma, multiple sclerosis, cancer, and chronic and extreme pain (Painter, 2024). The American Nurses Association (ANA) issued a position statement in support of evidence-based therapeutic use of marijuana and related cannabinoids for medical purposes (ANA Ethics Advisory Board, 2022). The ANA has requested a reevaluation and reclassification of marijuana's federal Schedule I controlled substance status. They suggest that it be relisted as a Schedule II controlled substance to enable much-needed clinical research. One should note that the adverse effects of marijuana include rapid heartbeat, some loss of coordination, and impaired immediate memory. The drugs can also adversely affect one's critical skills, including skills necessary to operate a vehicle safely, such as judgment of distance and reaction time.

The National Institutes of Health (NIH) published a finding by an expert panel in 1997 to investigate the therapeutical value of marijuana and identify the most valuable areas for future research direction (National Institutes of Health, 1997). The group identified the following five areas: (1) stimulates appetite and alleviates cachexia, (2) controls nausea and vomiting due to cancer-related chemotherapy, (3) reduces intraocular pressure in glaucoma, (4) analgesia, and (5) relieves neurologic and movement disorders. The group concluded that more extensive studies were needed to evaluate the potential of marijuana as supportive care for cancer. The suggested areas of study were a smoke-free delivery system of THC (marijuana's active ingredient), the effects of marijuana on the lungs and immune system, and the dangerous byproducts of smoked marijuana.

In 1999, another panel of experts at the Institute of Medicine released the most comprehensive analysis of the medical use of marijuana. This group cautioned that the benefits of smoking marijuana were limited because the smoke in itself is toxic (Stolberg, 1999). They also recommended that marijuana be given on a short-term basis and under close supervision to patients who did not respond to other therapies. As a result of the 1999 medical finding, seven states have legalized the use of medical cannabis. The US Supreme Court voted that despite the irony, Congress had the legal authority to make the use of homegrown marijuana a criminal offense, even in states where it is legal for therapeutic purposes. As a consequence, individuals and families who use or access medical cannabis in states that permit it are still vulnerable to criminal consequences.

Ethical Issues

The ethical dilemma that surrounds the debate on medical marijuana focuses on whether the Federal ban on the use of medical marijuana violates the physician–patient relationship. Is it ethical for physicians to prescribe medical marijuana to their patients as a medical treatment? There are two contrasting views. Recent studies suggest that medical marijuana is more effective than traditional FDA-approved medications in controlling pain and nausea from chemotherapy treatment, as well as in boosting the appetites of AIDS patients to combat wasting (Clarke, 2000). A direct violation of the physician–patient relationship is to deny physicians the right to discuss, recommend, and prescribe marijuana to patients. Physicians are responsible for providing adequate relief from pain and suffering to give patients an acceptable quality of life. Failure to provide an available treatment that has proven effective would violate the fundamental ethical principle of non-maleficence, which prohibits the infliction of harm, injury, or death (Clarke, 2000).

In contrast, as discussed earlier, there is a lack of clinical trials and patent protection for medical cannabis; some argue that these have put physicians in an ethical dilemma as relevant clinical data is missing for many health conditions. In many cases, physicians are legally required to prescribe a more costly and less effective drug. Furthermore, since there is a lack of good quality data concerning "the efficacy, dose-dependent curve, drug interactions, expected adverse effects and safety of the commercially available medical cannabis products," physicians can only prescribe any vague indications rather than evidence-based conditions (Sagy et al., 2018). These gaps may impair the physicians' decisions in customizing the therapy for each patient. Furthermore, because medical cannabis is classified as a Schedule I drug, instead of prescribing it, the physicians can issue a certificate for its use. Since physicians are required to discuss with patients the potential benefits and risks upon prescribing any medications, there is an unavoidable knowledge gap since the dosing and potency of medical cannabis are not regulated. Moreover, insufficient data on the long-term effects of cannabis use can impact the decision-making of both doctors and patients (Sagy et al., 2018).

Patients have the right to receive complete information and discuss all available treatment options with their physicians to make an informed decision about their treatments. If physicians fail, they violate the patient's right to informed consent (Annas, 1997). However, the "knowledge gaps" discussed above may impair the patient's ability to reach a fully informed decision. Some, therefore, argue that the lack of sufficient knowledge may lead to undesirable patient harm, which once again violates the physician's principle of non-maleficence. However, since the majority of patients prefer smoking medical cannabis over other methods, their right to autonomy interferes with the no-harm principle (Sagy et al., 2018).

Spill-Over Effects on Other Health Safety Issues

In 1999, the Institute of Medicine again published a report stating that there was no evidence suggesting that medical marijuana use would lead to more illicit drug use in the general population. The report also concluded that marijuana was not a "gateway drug" that would inevitably result in the use of other drugs like heroin or cocaine. Nevertheless, some individuals may perceive the legalization of medical marijuana as an endorsement of recreational drug use. A decade after the release of the report, another study raised concern that the dispensaries may be the source of increased commercial distribution of cannabis to the entire public rather than to those who have relevant health concerns (Thurstone, Lieberman & Schmiege, 2011). It was reported that 40 percent of teenagers receive marijuana from someone with a medical cannabis certificate. The study implies that patients with approved merchandise may pass or trade it with an unauthorized third party. The exposure to medical cannabis was found to be related to the availability of any cannabis and higher frequency of use, especially among teenagers. The finding has led some to conclude that the use of legalized substances such as cannabis may account for a more significant burden than other illegal drugs due to their widespread use rather than their actual harms (Sagy et al., 2018).

Legalizing medical marijuana is not primarily intended to encourage its recreational use. Its primary purpose is to alleviate the pain and discomfort that cannot be relieved by currently approved treatments or medications. According to Clarke (2000), thousands of patients who have illegally used marijuana for medical purposes have attested to its effectiveness. It may be considered morally acceptable by society to legalize the use of marijuana for patients who fail to respond to conventional treatments, as per the Federal government's regulations. Based on scientific research, the benefits of medical marijuana are far more significant than its drawbacks. Moreover, recent studies have shown that one reason public opinion has become more tolerant of physician-assisted suicide is that medical professionals have not adequately managed the pain and suffering of those with terminal diseases. Medical marijuana has been proven to be another valuable therapy or medical necessity for some with terminal illnesses. The fight against drug abuse is vital because many lives are lost to drug addiction. However, the battle against the effects of devastating diseases impacts a substantially more significant number of Americans (Clarke, 2000). It is equally important to bear in mind that while the policy is rapidly moving toward the legalization of cannabis and expanding the use of medical cannabis, there are still some ethical considerations that need to be ironed out along the way.

10

The Larger Impacts of Medical Tourism

The book will not be complete without discussing the larger impacts of medical tourism worldwide and on the home front. We divide the final chapter of the book into three broad sections. The first section deals with the impacts of medical tourism on destination countries, including favorable government policies, trickle-down economic development, and the effects on destination healthcare systems. The second section discusses the impacts of medical tourism on home countries—politically, socially, and financially—and especially its implications on home healthcare systems. The last section examines the current and future regulation of medical tourism worldwide.

Impacts on Destination Countries

Will the growing number of medical tourists from advanced economies seeking health care in destination countries, mainly developing ones, affect destination economies and their residents? If so, how? We will begin by looking at government initiatives on medical tourism in some of these destination countries, followed by the optimistic notion of trickle-down economic development in these economies, and, finally, the impacts of medical tourism on their healthcare systems.

Favorable Government Policies

Regional and national governments in India, Malaysia, Singapore, Thailand, the Philippines, and South Korea regard medical tourism as essential for economic and social development. The revenues generated from medical tourism significantly impact the economies of these Asian countries. The regional leaders consider the integration of tourism and healthcare industries as a critical channel for diversifying their economies, attracting foreign investments, promoting job creation, reinforcing the healthcare industry, and benefiting from the comparative advantage in the region (Turner, 2007).

Some of these destination countries began investing and improving their medical facilities and management stock to prepare for medical tourism. These investments include constructing new facilities, obtaining international accreditation, acquiring the latest medical equipment, and training and retaining doctors and nurses. Some destination governments also offer subsidies and tax incentives to participating private hospitals.

Singapore launched its Singapore Medicine—a multiagency public–private collaboration in 2003—intending to make the island country a regional hub of medical excellence. Similar initiatives emerged in other destination countries, including the Malaysia Healthcare Travel Council, the Philippine Medical Tourism Program, and the Korea International Medical Association, to name a few. These consortia are usually joint ventures between notable organizations formed by destination governments, various hospitals, and professional associations in the private sector (Ormond & Mainil, 2015). The government of Thailand began promoting medical tourism to overseas markets in 2004, after some policy revisions and the setting up of a website by the Tourism Authority of Thailand. The website supports treatment types, hospital locations, destination guides, and promotional packages from hospitals and travel agencies. India promoted medical tourism as early as 2002; its government reduced the import duties on medical equipment and issued a unique medical visa that allows medical tourists to stay up to a year to obtain medical treatment. In positioning itself as a global medical and wellness tourism hub, India launched a one-stop online portal called the "Heal in India" initiative. Medical tourists can locate a list of Indian healthcare providers, treatment costs, medical visa applications, redressal of grievances, and feedback. Jordan has a similar virtual portal for medical tourists called Salamtak or "your health" or "get well soon" in English, launched during the Covid-19 pandemic in 2020 to allow better communication and continuity of care between medical tourists and Jordanian private hospitals.

Trickle-Down Economic Development

The effects of trickle-down economics caused by medical tourism and its related benefits to the healthcare systems of the destination economies are undeniable. Medical tourism serves as a significant source of foreign exchange and employment generation for other associated industries such as tourism, hotels, restaurants, airlines, pharmaceuticals, and medical research, thus boosting the gross domestic product of these developing economies (Ramirez de Arellano, 2007; Turner, 2007).

Medical tourists often travel with their companions, who require accommodation, dining, transportation, banking, local sightseeing, and other services. In addition to seeking a single healthcare provider, medical tourists and their companions also seek related networks and infrastructure during their stays in the destination countries. Various industries like health care, hospitality, transportation, and airlines create a robust ecosystem supporting and enhancing medical tourists' overall experience. The destination economies can leverage trickle-down economics by developing effective strategies to position themselves as leading hubs for medical tourism. A comprehensive ecosystem-based approach guarantees that all stakeholders benefit, creating a sustainable and mutually beneficial environment for medical tourists and local economies. Medical tourism can boost the local economies and provide a promising future source of income. A case in point was when Thailand's Bumrungrad Hospital brought in 600,000 international patients in 2004 and helped the Thai economy through the Asian financial crisis of 1997 (Burkett, 2007).

Impacts on Destination Healthcare Systems

Trickle-down economics aside, the influx of medical tourists from advanced economies into developing economies to seek care invariably impacts the local healthcare system and its residents. In the following section, we will examine some of these direct and indirect impacts, whether positive or negative.

Minimizing External Brain Drain

The influx of revenues from the medical tourism industry will undoubtedly bolster the healthcare industry in destination economies. The benefits come in more than one way. First, the revenues can be reinvested into the economies to create long-term, high-skilled jobs necessary for a solid tertiary healthcare system (Whittaker, 2008). The better trained, higher salary, and high-tech work environment incentivize local doctors and health professionals to stay home, thus reducing the external brain drain process. Second, the newly constructed healthcare infrastructure can better serve international and local patients, who otherwise would have limited access to modern medical facilities and advanced medical technologies. Third, investment into advanced medical technologies will encourage locals who would otherwise travel abroad to get care at home, keeping financial capital within the country.

Fourth, the revenues earned from medical tourism may also allow developing countries to repatriate healthcare professionals, who accounted for a significant fraction of the physician and registered nurse workforce, for instance, in the United States (Mattoon & Rathindran, 2006). Assuming the remunerations thus earned are sent back to support their families in the developing economies, such practice is a positive spillover effect of external brain drain that will benefit developing economies.

Advanced Medical Technologies and Sharing of Knowledge Base

As medical tourism emerged, hospitals from destination economies began to invest heavily in "cutting-edge" or "state-of-the-art" medical equipment and devices. Indeed, better high-tech medical equipment tends to create trust in destination hospitals and among medical tourists. Approximately 12,000 firms worldwide produced and sold medical equipment, generating revenues exceeding $50 billion (Medical Tourism Magazine, 2010). Some well-known ones are GE Medical Systems, Siemens Healthcare, Hill-Rom, and Varian, whose sales have increased tremendously in recent years. Between 2003 and 2007, the United States sold more equipment to countries engaging in medical tourism than advanced economies like Belgium, Canada, Germany, Japan, and Switzerland (Medical Tourism Magazine, 2010). Latin America's most significant equipment importers are Brazil, Chile, Mexico, and Venezuela, accounting for three-quarters of the regional market share. Brazil alone had 25 percent growth in 2008, importing 34 percent of the regional share. Between 2002 and 2018, Turkish public hospitals acquired nearly 6,000 ultrasounds, 73 linear accelerators, 37 PETs and CTs, and 9 tomotherapy (International Trade Administration, 2024). Nearly 80 percent of Turkey's medical devices are imported.

According to a Brazilian source, the materials, equipment, medicines, and diagnostics industry generated 2,100 new jobs in the first quarter of 2010, which was 6.9 percent higher than the same period in the previous year (Medical Tourism Magazine, 2010). The acquisition of new equipment also resulted in the hiring of skilled labor in Brazil.

Furthermore, some US hospitals with an international presence are known to share their medical management protocols with their affiliated hospitals in destination economies. For instance, Johns Hopkins has developed consulting and referral relationships with its affiliated hospitals in Turkey, India, and Singapore. In the case of Anadolu Medical Center in Turkey, the collaboration allows the hospital to contact specialists from Johns Hopkins for second opinions and teleconference briefings (Inci, 2012). Sharing medical knowledge will benefit medical tourists and the local population.

Increased Competition for Healthcare Resources

Does medical tourism limit care access for residents in destination countries? One prevailing argument is that medical tourism depletes or competes with the healthcare resources of destination economies. There are two types of competition for healthcare resources. The first type of competition is international—between medical tourists from advanced economies and residents of developing economies. The second type of competition is intranational—between the affluent and poor residents of developing economies. Either type of competition has raised health equity issues.

The influx of medical tourists to developing countries has positive and negative outcomes on the local health systems. On the one hand, the inflow of revenues into local health care, tourism, and hospitality industries will ideally be channeled through the economy to improve health care for the local population, but this is often not the case. In Thailand and India, there are only nine and seven doctors per ten thousand people in 2020 (World Health Organization, 2024). This is significantly lower than the average of 17 per 10,000 people globally or twenty-eight per ten thousand in the United States. Thailand and India are hotspots for medical tourism, and medical tourists may take these doctors and health resources from locals because it is more lucrative to treat them. One view is that medical tourists compete with resources with residents and use more than the average resident would use. In Thailand, one medical tourist uses approximately the exact cost of resources to treat four to five local patients (Chen & Flood, 2013).

To attract medical tourists, hospitals from developing economies often invest heavily in costly diagnostic imaging devices and advanced biomedical technologies. Because medical tourists tend to travel for treatments that often require advanced biomedical technologies rather than routine care, the medical tourism industry means focusing more on high-tech biomedicine over prevention. Since the residents often cannot afford access to these technologies, it means promoting technology-intensive tertiary services at the expense of primary care and public health (Wilson, 2009).

In the case of the Philippines, a group of doctors opposed the government initiative on medical tourism, criticizing the practice, which will further marginalize poor local patients and significantly reduce services available to charity patients (Gahlinger, 2008). However, these fears turned out to be unfounded. The truth was that there has been a significant increase in the number of hospitals, clinics, doctors, healthcare staff, and ancillary services because of considerable investments in the medical tourism industry. There has been an influx of local healthcare professionals to their countries instead of losing them to emigration—a reversal of brain drain. These professionals have more opportunities to stay at home to serve both the medical tourists and the locals. A single new hospital can employ 3,000 nurses and other ancillary medical staff who otherwise would have been unemployed.

Health Equity, Social Justice, and Political Sovereignty

Since most medical tourism destinations are developing economies, opponents of medical tourism highlight social and political issues such as health equity, social justice, and the political sovereignty of these economies. They argued that medical tourism has limited the access of the local population to healthcare professionals and facilities (Hazarika, 2009; Vijaya, 2010), thus affecting the political sovereignty of the destination economy (Burkett, 2007). More specifically, from these economies' perspective, some were concerned whether the more "affluent" international patients would constrain the resources of the local communities, making quality health care less affordable for the less affluent local patients (Hazarika, 2009; Vijaya, 2010). Another reiterated that the rising demand for quality medical care by an increasingly large number of medical tourists could drive up the cost of providing primary health care for everyone, including the locals, making it less affordable for them (Turner, 2007). This is incredibly inequitable given that essential medical services are prohibitively expensive or simply unavailable for the population in some of these destination countries. Under the Indian government initiative, the newly constructed private hospitals must agree to a dual pricing system that offers lower prices to domestic patients (Chinai & Goswami, 2007). However, this rarely happened in reality.

Aggravation of Internal Brain Drain

We will look at the second type of intranational competition in healthcare resources, which is leading to serious health equity issues. Some developing countries, such as Thailand and India, have voiced concerns regarding resource and brain drain from the underfunded and understaffed public hospitals in rural areas to private for-profit hospitals in urban areas, resulting in a two-tier system for healthcare delivery (Hazarika, 2009). The prospects of treating high-paying medical tourists and having access to modern facilities and advanced medical technologies while receiving a higher wage are all incredible incentives for public healthcare professionals in rural areas to make the move. The migration of these healthcare professionals from public hospitals to private ones has left the already struggling public health systems even more understaffed. The two-tier system may increase the inequality in healthcare access between private and public systems, with dissimilar standards for different economic classes (Ramirez de Arellano, 2007). In some cases, a significant amount of public funds was used to support building private hospitals catering to affluent locals and medical tourists. Although the government initially supported medical tourism, with the understanding that the new private healthcare facilities would reserve some beds to care for low-income residents, it rarely happened (Thomas & Krishnan, 2010).

There are conflicting reports to support the argument that medical tourism will result in a two-tier healthcare system in the destination economies. We will examine the proportion of healthcare expenditure in both public and private sectors in Thailand and India. The Thai public health expenditure declined from 36 percent of total health expenditure in 2004 to 27 percent in 2021, and its private health expenditure increased proportionately over the same period (World Bank Group, 2024a). Thus, there may be some justification to support the argument for the two-tier system in the case of Thailand. In contrast, the Indian public health expenditure doubled from 18 percent of total health expenditure in 2004 to 36 percent in 2021. Its government expenditure on private health had been plummeting accordingly during the same period (World Bank Group, 2024b), thus debunking the two-tier system argument. Depending on each destination county, the health inequity caused by the two-tier system between the public and private health sectors may be overrated.

Impacts on Home Countries

So how does medical tourism impact these home countries, which are typically developed economies, particularly their healthcare systems and the poor?

Viewpoints and Guidelines from the AMA

How do the advanced nations and their medical professions view medical tourism? In 2006, the American Medical Association (AMA) issued a position statement regarding medical tourism (AMA, 2007). In general, nothing prevents American medical tourists from seeking care abroad. The gist of AMA's concerns focuses on assurance of continuity of care and post-care, that it will not burden the US healthcare system and that the third-party payers should exercise their responsibilities with foreign healthcare providers they contract with. They specifically advise insurers to choose providers who can guarantee the availability of reasonable follow-up care upon patients' return home. Further, regarding doctor's credentials and facilities, third-party payers should require the same quality of care comparable to those required in the United States. Further, the patients should be provided with appeals and legal rights similar to those of US-based healthcare providers, and they should be given the option to seek care in the United States.

Impacts on Home Healthcare Systems

Just like destination countries, advanced economies see opportunities and impediments in the practice of medical tourism. Developed economies such as the United States, which face an aging population and escalating healthcare costs, may view medical tourism as a feasible alternative to solve their healthcare problems. In economies with universal healthcare systems, such as the UK and Canada, medical tourism has been lauded as a solution to reduce long surgical wait lists.

Reactions and Creative Innovations

From a bigger political perspective, there is greater consumer sovereignty in allowing medical tourism to flourish. On the other hand, the high volume of patient outflow to foreign countries represents a substantial loss of revenues for the domestic healthcare professions and, eventually, the domestic healthcare systems. The outflow of patients may bring about resistance among healthcare professionals at home. They may refuse to participate in a Preferred Provider Network that includes foreign providers or boycott insurance companies that cover international treatments by denying services to their members.

The trend of international medical tourism may also lead to creative structural changes and the offering of specialized treatments among domestic healthcare providers. For instance, they may specialize in bundle care for specific procedures by conducting them in high quality and volumes, thus allowing them to offer rates at a deep discount. A case in point is Galichia Heart Hospital in Wichita, Kansas, which offered a flat fee of $10,000 for coronary artery bypass graft (CABG) without complication in 2008—a price comparable with those offered by popular destination countries. As of 2024, their price for CABG at Galichia ranged from $46,000 to $127,000 or a median price of $74,000. Its median price is more than three times lower than the US median price of $247,000. However, it is three times higher than the Mexican price and only slightly more than one and a half times higher than the price in Singapore. The initial flat fee offered by Galichia Heart Hospital was intended to keep US patients and, eventually, the healthcare revenues within the domestic healthcare system.

Continuity of Care

Other medical and financial impacts on domestic healthcare systems evolve mainly around continuity of care and post-surgical complications. Specific ethical and moral issues may arise throughout the medical tourist's healing journey. They may come in the form of medical complications because of procedures performed by a foreign doctor and, subsequently, imposing additional responsibility on a domestic doctor to care for the patient. A domestic healthcare system may be affected adversely because of this. For instance, complications from cosmetic surgeries often require hospital admission, surgical intervention, and long-term follow-up in the home countries, all of which can pose a substantial financial burden that ranges between $26,000 and $154,000 (ISAPS, 2021). The lack of proper post-care requires patients to be evaluated by a new US medical team that is unknown to patients, which has resulted in unnecessary diagnostic testing and interventions. It cost the US healthcare system an estimated $1.3 billion to treat complications from medical tourists in 2017 (Adabi et al., 2017). In Australia, treating a severely infected joint arthroplasty performed abroad has led to nine times the cost of what it would have been had the procedure been conducted in a domestic facility (Cheung & Wilson, 2007). Similarly, in the UK, the wait time to treat other more acute and emergent procedures, such as oncology and trauma, has increased in the National Health Services, all because of treating complications resulting from plastic surgeries performed by doctors outside the country (Jeevan & Armstrong, 2008).

The Poor in Developed Economies

For the most part, medical tourism involves elective treatment, not emergent procedures requiring immediate lifesaving attention. As Milstein and Smith (2006) put it, "to ensure significant savings excluding travel expenses and patients' safety, such offshore care must be restricted to non-urgent, short-duration treatments costing more than $15,000 to $20,000 in the United States for conditions not aggravated by air travel." Medical tourism does not apply to all medical procedures and does not meet all patients' needs.

What about the poor in advanced economies? Can they access medical tourism? Can they afford, for instance, $15,000 to $20,000 out-of-pocket expenditure? Currently, publicly funded insurance in the United States, such as Medicare or Medicaid, does not cover treatments abroad unless it is an emergency while members travel abroad. However, in some countries with publicly funded healthcare systems, such as Canada, patients may be able to opt for elective care abroad. It was reported that a small percentage of Canadian medical tourists could get reimbursement from their public Medicare system if they could prove that the care was medically necessary and that they could not receive timely care in Canada (Eggertson, 2006). However, medical tourism becomes possible only for those who can afford to pay out-of-pocket before departure. If the poor in the advanced economies cannot travel outside the countries for care, does medical tourism cherry-pick patients, leaving the very poorest at home? Does medical tourism lead to inequality in access to universal health care? Like health inequity issues discussed earlier in developing economies, these questions raise similar concerns over social justice and universal health equity, something for health policymakers in advanced nations to ponder.

Long-Term Impacts

On a brighter note, the emergence of medical tourism may pressure some US healthcare providers to reduce prices, as in the case of Galichia Heart Hospital in Wichita, Kansas. It may force greater transparency in pricing and surgical outcomes and an upgrade to more efficient healthcare delivery methods in the domestic healthcare system (York, 2008). However, to compete, the pressure to lower the price may result in longer wait lines and lower quality care due to less time spent by some domestic doctors. Worse, it may even reduce the number of potential doctors willing to enter the profession, adversely affecting patient care.

Future Regulation of Medical Tourism

Medical tourism has often been described as the "Wild West" in terms of its regulatory environment. Regarding regulation, medical tourism is an industry to watch since it has the potential to stimulate general tourism, hospitality, infrastructure, and more as a significant means for economic growth.

Two ideas regarding the ethicality of medical tourism are very apparent: regulation of medical tourism for the safety of medical tourists and regulation of medical tourism to protect the local population. Medical tourism is a lucrative industry, but to ensure that it is a win-win situation for everyone, there needs to be regulation. Host or destination governments should enact laws that require facilities to be up to par with global standards. This would mean a clean, sterile environment with qualified professionals. Above all, the local population should be prioritized. There should be enough medical resources available for every resident. Medical tourism is a private business, so local governments should implement taxation to benefit the public. Medical tourism can be advantageous for everyone involved, but it is up to local governments to ensure it is regulated. Without regulation, there would be chaos among the public and private health sectors. "Without regulation, the potential positive effects may not be realized, and medical tourism may contribute to a harmful global commodification of healthcare." (Johnston et al., 2010).

Some maintained that attracting patients to countries such as India and Thailand could increase regional economic inequalities and undermine health equity (Turner, 2007). As the medical tourism industry grows, a policy implication is for government officials to add regulations to their medical tourism industries, especially around healthcare equity for medical tourists and residents in low- and middle-income countries. To avoid a two-tier healthcare administration with treatment disparities between the local populous and medical tourists, Chen & Flood (2013) contended that governments should regulate the medical tourism industry present in their jurisdiction. They also mentioned that "beneficial healthcare spillovers and trickle-down economics in this industry have yet to be significantly realized despite substantial promotion and the allocation of public resources for medical tourism."

Many developing economies face governance and regulatory failures, which creates a prevalent obstacle in creating medical tourism regulation and policy implementation. Therefore, some argued that policymakers from wealthier countries should consider assisting developing economies with their infrastructure around medical tourism. The reason is that poorer countries may encounter adverse effects of the industry due to poor policy choices. All countries should anticipate challenges in navigating regulations. However, international collaboration will be a great help considering the global interest.

A study in Guatemala reiterated that regulating the medical tourism industry should promote a safe place for medical tourists and focus on residents. The study favors the Ministry of Health as the unit that regulates the industry. The appropriate ministry will emphasize safety, stricter requirements for medical professionals, and ensure resources are not hoarded in the private medical tourism business (Labonté et al., 2018). The authors proposed that the medical tourism industry should be taxed effectively due to the cost of resources that medical tourists consume. The proceeds should be plowed back to benefit the local infrastructure and redistributed to fund healthcare access for the poor. To do that, there needs to be the setting up of primary health clinics in underserved regions and private hospitals offering some level of free service for the locals (Johnston et al., 2010).

In another study on imposing local regulation on the medical tourism industry in Barbados, a group of local lawyers said that to minimize any adverse effects on Barbados's reputation, especially in dealing with medical malpractice cases, the government needed to consider laws, licensing, liability, and ownership of medical tourism businesses (Crooks et al., 2015) and eventually develop a solid medical malpractice law.

Although the need to regulate the medical tourism industry has been voiced in developing economies such as India, Guatemala, Barbados, and many others, supporting regulatory guidelines should also be in place in home countries. As mentioned earlier, the United States has general guidelines concerning medical tourism, which were issued by the AMA in 2006. However, some raise concerns that countries where medical tourists originate, such as Australia and Canada, do not have existing national guidelines for patients' or home doctors' participation in medical tourism (Crooks & Snyder, 2010). These guidelines are necessary to protect medical tourists from patient safety issues, adequate post-care responses in home healthcare systems, and unethical promotional sales pitches. For instance, developing stronger malpractice laws in destination countries could significantly improve patient safety issues and better informational and care coordination tools among domestic countries (Johnston et al., 2010). The long-term goal should include a comprehensive international approach that requires guidelines to be in place in both destination and home countries.

Final Words

It has been reported that the United States spends more on health care as a percentage of its GDP than any other country. In 2022, the US spent 17.8 percent of its GDP on health care or twice as much as the average OECD country (Gunja, Gumas & Williams, 2023). There are numerous reasons behind the rising healthcare costs in the United States. One is defensive medicine, which is the practice of overusing unnecessary medical procedures due to the fear of malpractice litigation (Roethberg et al., 2014). Another cause is medical consumerism. This is when patients demand a higher usage of prescription drugs and take advantage of medical breakthroughs and the newest medical technology even though they gain no real advantage (Thorpe, 2005). It is also believed that the rising healthcare costs are due to a lack of competition in the healthcare market and a lack of transparency in the patient–doctor relationship (Beck, 2014).

Domestic doctors can undoubtedly do something concerning the lack of transparency in their relationship with patients. The style of American care has been described as "many referrals and tests, impersonal doctor-patient relationships, uniform treatment protocols, and overreliance on surgery" (Horton & Cole, 2011). American physicians worried about the expansion of medical tourism have two options: they can criticize and try to limit it or take the lead and endorse initiatives to accelerate the development and adoption of more effective domestic healthcare delivery practices (Milstein & Smith, 2006). A report by the Institute of Medicine in 2005 discussed the use of systems engineering methods in delivering health care. One source estimated that approximately 30 percent to 40 percent of healthcare spending in the United States at that time was being wasted. This wastage was mainly attributed to the delivery of services that were unlikely to improve patients' health status or satisfaction and the inefficient provision of valuable services.

To relieve some of those claims, domestic or home doctors in advanced economies can play an essential role in helping medical tourists overcome the quality-of-care barriers (Gan & Frederick, 2018). Social ties and trust in medical professionals and their recommendations often influence patients' choice of destination hospitals (Gooding, 1995; Javalgi, Rao, and Thomas, 1991). Further, domestic doctors are typically well-informed about up-to-date medical technology and procedures; they can better assess surgical outcomes, foreign doctors' credentials, and JCI accreditation standards. Thus, they are better positioned to recommend appropriate treatments for specific diseases and conditions. Moreover, if they recommend and refer a patient internationally, they certainly would be happy to assume the responsibility for the continuity of care upon the patient's return.

From the institutional perspective of advanced economies, proponents of medical tourism maintain that keeping the option of a lower-cost offshore healthcare alternative allows medical tourists to access quality care and relieves the strain on public resources for the sick and uninsured at home, especially in the United States. From economic and social viewpoints, outsourcing elective health care will reduce the demand pressure in the healthcare system of advanced economies and allow the latter to serve the urgent healthcare demand of aging baby boomers, for instance, in long-term care and quality of life in retirement homes. All these may result in more excellent partnerships between domestic and destination healthcare providers through affiliation agreements or formal patient referrals.

Finally, integrative medicine is the emerging healthcare focus and delivery model expected to continue well into the future among all ages in the United States and globally. Integrative medicine integrates alternative and wellness approaches into mainstream medicine, something the European nations have long embraced as "health tourism" or "wellness tourism." Wellness tourism includes spa services such as yoga, massage, acupuncture, Ayurveda, aromatic and herbal therapies, and thermal springs. As indicated in Chapter 3, the fact that the CAM 2017 survey showed a drastic surge of interest in meditation and yoga among the seventeen–years-old or younger Americans is a testimony that the younger generations are learning to embrace natural healing approaches for their body, mind, and spirit. This is especially comforting knowing that an estimated 50 percent of US teenagers have faced serious mental illnesses, anxiety, and depressions at some point in their lives (USDHHS-NIMH, 2021). The niche market of health and wellness tourism is expected to grow alongside medical tourism. It will help drive the mainstream medical tourism market for the coming decades. As York (2008) puts it, "the brave new world of globalized medicine could provide an open market exchange of medical innovations, information, and exciting advancements both in the United States and abroad."

Welcome to the brave new world of globalized medicine. As the book concludes, your healing journey has just begun.

Part III

Scenarios

Case 1

Bob Needs Assurance of Patient Safety

Bob is self-employed and does not have health insurance. Bob and his wife Sarah are struggling with a decision on whether to travel to India for his coronary artery bypass graft surgery (CABG), which can cost $250,000 in the United States but only $12,000 in India. Low cost does not mean low quality. They have read about the doctors' good credentials, the affiliation of some big-name US hospitals in India, and the attentiveness of nurses in a one-to-one nurse–patient ratio. They all sound so good. Sarah has also read about the traditional Indian Ayurvedic treatment involving yoga and relaxation, which may complement Bob's surgery nicely. Yet they are still uncertain about the quality of care Bob may receive in addition to safety concerns when traveling to a developing country with a different culture from theirs. Even though English is widely spoken in big cities such as Mumbai, which is where they plan to go, the Indian diet is a lot spicier than the standard American diet. Can they overcome the diverse cultural differences and travel to India for care?

Analysis

Bob is among the existing twenty-five million US uninsured persons who aspire to travel abroad for care primarily due to the phenomenal cost savings, especially for big-ticket treatments such as CABG. Bob's concerns are probably the most frequently asked questions among medical tourists—the assurance of patient safety. This boils down to the perception of quality of care in the destination country and the hospital. Bob and Sarah will be experiencing a new climate that is hot and humid, and they may be exposed to new strains of virus, bacteria, or fungus while traveling on a long-haul flight to India. For starters, they should check the travel advisories put out by the US Department of State (travel.state.gov) regarding India before deciding on the country. They should also check the

CDC website for recent warnings on cases of American medical tourists who suffered from any treatments in particular facilities in India.

Like many potential medical tourists, Bob and Sarah may have certain perceptions of a destination country, especially if it is a developing or third-world country such as India. They are familiar with the American care environment, how medical needs are being taken care of, and the general quality of care in the United States. One perception is that the hospital staff in developing countries may not have a high awareness of sanitation. Thus, patients may be more susceptible to severe disease infection from the hospital. Therefore, choosing a reputable hospital with JCI accreditation or a US-affiliated medical center is strongly recommended. And there are many such facilities in India. In addition, they should look into the surgeon's credentials in advance, for instance, where the surgeon receives his medical education, training, and clinical specialty. They should also be aware of hospital website reviews by previous patients, as these can be easily fabricated to make the facility or the doctor look better. Even if online reviews are accurate, one good surgery does not necessarily extend to all surgeries with the same outcome. Individual patients have different medical histories and health conditions. They may be treated differently from others who have undergone the same procedure at the same facility.

Further, even though doctors and hospital staff speak English in India, it may be spoken less widely outside the hospital. It will be Bob and Sarah's first trip to India, and they plan to contact the hospital directly rather than the service of a facilitator. Given that they are traveling to India for the first time, coupled with possible language and cultural barriers, it is highly recommended that they investigate in a hospital with a strong presence of an international patient center (IPC). Preferably, it will fill the role of a facilitating agent. Ideally, the IPC will fulfill concierge services such as having a hospital staff meet them at the airport, arranging for her accommodation and local transportation, and advising on local shopping, dining, and banking needs. Suppose a spicy Indian diet is their concern. In that case, they may want to communicate their diet needs to the hospital in advance so some Western food may be catered to during their stay in India. The IPC may also arrange a separate Ayurvedic relaxation treatment during Bob's recovery period. Such alternative therapy not only will enhance both of their well-being, but it will also take the stress out from having treatments in a foreign country.

Given that CABG is a major elective surgery, the continuity of care is a valid concern, and they should certainly watch out for hidden costs. Suppose Bob plans to have his follow-up care in the United States. In that case, he should communicate and schedule that with his home doctor before leaving for India. Any unexpected postopearative care with complications and side effects can defeat their cost savings. Bob may require additional treatment after returning to the United States, which could cost them an arm and a leg. Further, he may face significant costs of emergency evacuation to the United States if there are complications, and their travel insurance may not cover this. Bob is therefore highly recommended to purchase both complications and travel insurance.

To overcome the problem of third-world country perception and cultural differences, Bob and Sarah will need to assess their tradeoffs honestly. Cost savings are a primary concern for uninsured people, who may have limited choices outside India. However, cultural similarity is an important consideration. In that case, they may want to compromise treatment costs and choose a country with a slightly similar culture, such as Portugal, Spain, Ukraine, or Mexico. These destination countries advertise comparable prices for the same procedure, although not as low as India. However, they have done adequate research and prepared themselves. In that case, they may convince themselves they can overcome cultural perceptions and differences. Going to India may be the best decision they have made for Bob.

Case 2

How Would Judy Choose a Facilitator?

Due to a shorter waitlist, Judy wishes to get a knee replacement done outside the United States. She has always wanted to take a dream vacation in Turkey even though she had never traveled abroad. Being inundated with so many medical and travel decisions, Judy used a medical tourism agent in the United States to help her source a healthcare provider in Turkey. But which agent would she choose in the first place? Can she trust any agents she looks up on the Internet with such an important decision? What are some selection criteria when it comes to choosing the middleman? How does she pay, and at what point of the journey? What is the scope of services the agent provides, and what are the agent's responsibilities if something goes wrong? She does not know anyone who has used the middleman service besides those who share testimonials on the facilitating company's websites. She is also unaware that the medical tourism agent business is unregulated.

Analysis

Due to asymmetric information and high search costs, the average potential medical tourist like Judy knows little about destination countries and the services provided by their hospitals. She decides to hire a medical tourism facilitator. Chapter 4 presents the essential selection criteria of a facilitator and points out that they can vary significantly from one agent to another. Most of them have knowledge of the industry, but can they be trusted? Chapter 7 highlights that most agents' websites emphasize a wide range of services they provide, but there is little evidence of pricing transparency or company-related information, such as the companies' history or the management team's background. Though the website information appears impressive, if not overwhelming, Judy knows very little about the company and the man behind it.

At the minimum, Judy should look for an agent with transparent pricing for travel coordination, including airport transfers, accommodations, and related concierge services provided in her destination country. Judy should also choose a more established agent who refers her to a reputable hospital based on accreditation, low nurse–patient ratios, good doctor credentials, and advanced medical technology. More importantly, she should seek one that communicates potential surgical risks, post-care responsibilities, and informed consent to her.

Chapter 5 has a detailed section on the pricing schemes of the agents. Some may charge an "all-inclusive" fixed price with bundled services; others may charge the ala carte style. Some may charge a flat concierge fee of $200–$500 in addition to the treatment costs, yet others may charge a percentage-based commission for services they help arrange. Some agents receive a referral fee directly from the foreign hospital. Judy should find out all these, especially what is included in a "package," before committing to any payment. She should consider purchasing travel and complications insurance if they are not included in the "package."

In addition, Judy should refrain from relying on patient testimonials on the agents' websites because these can be obtained selectively and with little cost, as pointed out in Chapters 5 and 7. Likewise, as mentioned in the earlier scenario, online reviews of hospitals can be easily fabricated to make the facility or the physician look good. Therefore, Judy should be aware and skeptical of such testimonials. Her best recommendation should come from satisfied friends and families who have used a particular agent or hospital with good outcomes.

Furthermore, Judy should be aware that the agents' industry is self-regulated. A few private organizations have attempted to "regulate" the industry by offering various certification programs. Still, the industry needs a strong industry-support model based on international standards and patient protection.

Moreover, medical negligence and malpractice should be major concerns for potential patients like Judy. What is the facilitators' fiduciary responsibility in case of malpractice? It is difficult to prove the agent has committed corporate negligence in most cases, let alone medical malpractice. As pointed out in Chapter 9, it requires patients to establish the physician's incompetence, the agent's knowledge of this incompetence, and a series of misconduct by the physician. Further, it is hard to determine whether greater oversight by the agent could have avoided medical negligence (Mirrer-Singer, 2007). The final recommendation to Judy is to exercise due diligence and carefully research a few agents before shortlisting one. Again, her best recommendation should come from satisfied friends and families who have used a particular agent or a specific hospital in Turkey with successful outcomes.

Case 3

Brian Wants to Sue

To preserve his privacy, Brian crossed the border from Texas to Mexico. He had a tummy tuck procedure done over the weekend. Still, Brian unexpectedly faced surgery complications and infections after his return. He tried to contact the clinic through email or phone but was either unanswered or unable to get through. His doctor in the United States was unwilling to fix some botched surgery done by another doctor abroad. Facing a real dilemma, Brian had to turn to the emergency room for his post-surgery complications. Soon, all his friends and relatives would find out about his procedure. In addition to enduring additional pains and suffering, Brian was enraged, and he seriously considered suing the foreign doctor in Mexico. But how would he even do it in an unfamiliar foreign legal system?

Analysis

The protection of privacy is one strong reason why so many American medical tourists like Brian cross the border to Mexico for treatment, especially in bariatric or cosmetic surgeries. However, when something went wrong, Brian had to turn to the emergency room (ER) in his home country to treat complications such as infections. Due to a lack of appropriate postoperative care, such complications usually require hospital admission, surgical intervention, and long-term follow-up. It can potentially pose a significant financial burden, ranging between $25,000 and $150,000. Unfortunately, Brian's complications will likely be evaluated at the ER without the supervision of a cosmetic surgeon initially. He might undergo some extensive and unnecessary diagnostic interventions before being referred to a cosmetic surgeon after his discharge. Further, Brian's recovery will take time, which could mean longer absenteeism from work than anticipated. Soon, his family, friends, and coworkers would find out about the procedure that has led to his current predicament.

If Brian decided to take his medical complications case to the next step by filing a malpractice suit against the Mexican clinic performing the procedure, things could become more complex. Brian's insurance company will not pay for the tummy tuck mainly because it is bariatric. As pointed out in Chapter 3, although there might be some exceptions if the patient is obese, it still requires preauthorization by his insurer. Since Brian took the trip by himself without the prior authorization of his insurance company, his insurance company is not directly involved or responsible for expenses related to medical complications. Therefore, Brian is up against the Mexican clinic himself.

As pointed out in Chapter 9, many destination countries are reluctant to deal with medical malpractice, and Mexico is no exception. While the average compensation for medical malpractice claims in the United States is around $330,000, the average payout for Mexico is only around $5,000. Brian does not speak Spanish; he may need to hire a Spanish-speaking lawyer to help him wade through the Mexican legal system. He may also need to make multiple trips to Mexico for court hearings and proceedings. Mexican court rulings may not be as efficient as in the United States. It may take years to resolve a malpractice lawsuit in Mexico. Mexican healthcare providers may not be as cooperative as in their non-communication through emails or phone attempts. They may even refuse to provide Biran's medical records. It can be challenging for Brian to prove what exactly happened. Further, finding a Mexican medical professional willing to testify on Brian's behalf is challenging.

As pointed out in Chapter 9, under the corporate negligence theory, the foreign clinic can be held responsible for negligently hiring or retaining incompetent doctors or failing to supervise them adequately (Mirrer-Singer, 2007). Additionally, a court hearing would likely apply the law of Mexico where the alleged malpractice occurred, and Mexico might not recognize the US corporate negligence law. Potential medical tourists should know that proving corporate negligence is complex and challenging. It requires a patient to establish the physician's incompetence and a pattern of misconduct by the physician (Mirrer-Singer, 2007).

Given all these facts, Brian could use a less formal and less expensive service of Comision National de Arbitraje Medico (Conamed). This alternative government agency handles malpractice cases through conciliation and arbitration. As highlighted in Chapter 9, this alternative service can speed up conflict resolution. The arbiter has typically more medical knowledge than a lawyer (Tena-Tamayo & Sotelo, 2005). It may take only three to six months for conciliation and fifteen months for sentencing. Due to the absence of lawyer fees and court costs, Brian's potential compensations may be lower than those awarded by a court. However, this may be precisely what Biran needs instead of going through a formal and more prolonged and cumbersome legal system in an unfamiliar country.

In Brian's case, not purchasing complications insurance before his trip is the lesson he learned. For some complications, insurance waives all deductibles and coinsurance. It covers between $15,000 and $50,000 within a year after the complications have taken place (Medical Tourism Corporation, 2024). Some "health travel" insurance policies cover extra medical expenses associated with complications, including additional consultations and hospital stays, and additional trip expenses, including airfare and accommodation, for up to a year.

Case 4

Logan Is Offered Incentives

Logan lives in Detroit, Michigan, and works for a car manufacturer in his city. He injured his shoulder while on the job and needed surgery. His company, a self-insured employer, opted to send him to Thailand for surgery and is willing to pay for an additional airfare of a companion, a bonus of $10,000 in addition to the treatment and travel costs to Thailand. He and his wife of forty years can always take a side trip to relax and recoup after his surgery at one of many Thai beaches, often featured in travel magazines. It sounds almost too good to believe. Would Logan go? Are there any repercussions that he should consider? After all, why would an American company be so willing to trust a foreign healthcare system over its domestic healthcare system? Are US insurers or employers legally allowed to send their employees overseas for treatment? Is cost the only reason? What about safety and quality?

Analysis

As presented in Chapter 8, Logan faces the same two vital questions third-party payers ask when contemplating whether to engage in medical tourism and promote its activities. These two questions are: Is it legal for employers to ask their workers to seek care abroad? What is the fiduciary responsibility of the employers in case of malpractice? Unless Logan resides in Texas, there is no state law in Michigan that would prevent its residents from traveling outside the country (or out of state) for treatment. As pointed out in Chapter 6, many US states, such as Florida, Rhode Island, and Minnesota, have set aside funds to promote interstate medical tourism as early as 2013. With the help of medical tourism agents, many employers have tried to negotiate for lower prices with many Midwestern hospitals, such as several in Kansas City and Oklahoma City. However, they still need to catch up compared to the surgery price in Thailand.

Cost is not the only reason companies send their employees abroad for care. Many employers have considered safety and quality of care after researching or working with a reputable medical tourism facilitator. They are looking for a JCI-accredited hospital with track records of good patient outcomes and satisfaction. They look beyond just the "excellent" testimonies published on the hospital website. Some employers have even taken a trip to the destination country and visited the hospital to inspect its safety and quality. That seems like a lot of research, but you are talking about the care and well-being of your employees. That is precisely what HSM Solutions, a furniture manufacturer based in North Carolina, has done. The director of benefits of HSM took the first trip to India with a worker who needed treatment in 2007. Since then, 250 employees and dependents have benefited from medical tourism. It has also saved the company around $20 million in healthcare expenditure during the first six years of implementing the idea of medical tourism.

So, would Logan go? Are there any repercussions that he should consider? Yes, there might be a slight chance of a potential boycott from the union representing car manufacturers, primarily due to its implication of possible job losses in the US healthcare industry. However, we are talking about other sectors, such as health care, instead of direct job losses in the relevant car manufacturing sector. The boycott is, at best, political; the impact on job losses is negligible, if any.

When it comes to the fiduciary responsibility of the employers in case of malpractice, there is hardly any potential legal liability on the part of Logan's company. Because Logan's employer is a self-funded insurer, the company acts as his insurer. It sets aside funds to cover medical claims and employee fees. A self-insured company is not subject to state law, and therefore, it is not liable in any malpractice lawsuit; in this case, the foreign hospital involved is more likely to be directly responsible.

Finally, would Logan go? He would probably go after having all his questions answered. After all, he is helping his company and fellow employees by taking the plunge. Assuming his treatment outcome is satisfactory will encourage more employees and their dependents to follow suit. They will save the company tons of dollars, which can then be reinvested into its healthcare expenditure and expand more offshore service offerings to benefit more employees. Logan's positive move is known as "positive externality" in economics. As pointed out at the end of Chapter 8, it is a win-win situation; not only will this help foster employees' loyalty and morale, but it also demonstrates a forward-thinking corporate culture that Logan is undoubtedly proud of.

Case 5

Cathy Does Not Want to Move Out of State

Cathy lives in North Carolina. She has stage four colon cancer and is undergoing chemotherapy. Cathy has learned that medical cannabis can alleviate chemo-related nausea, manage cancer pain effectively, and even reduce the growth of cancer tumors. To seek an alternative cancer treatment protocol using cannabis, she traveled to Virginia, a neighboring state in which the growth of the plant and the use of cannabis for medicinal purposes is legal, unlike her home state. Cathy was concerned that her insurance company may not reimburse her treatment cost since her treatment is considered a complementary and alternative therapy and, most of all, unapproved by the FDA. She went to her conventional doctor, who refused to prescribe her medical cannabis. Instead, they prescribed her expensive and less effective conventional medicine, which Cathy refused. The doctor finally agreed to sign a form attesting to her diagnosis but holds no responsibility as to where or how she might obtain the cannabis. With that form, Cathy was able to get a medical cannabis certificate online before driving across the state line to Virginia, four hours from her home. She was able to buy what she needed from Virginia. But before returning home, she was concerned whether it was legal to transport the products back to her home state to continue her treatment. If that is not possible, is it legal for her to order the products online and have them shipped to her home state? More importantly, in the medium to long run, where can she go to advocate her right to use cannabis in her home state other than simply moving to Virginia or other cannabis "friendly" states?

Analysis

As of July 2024, cannabis is still a controlled substance in the state of North Carolina, and possession of it is illegal. As pointed out in Chapter 6, cannabis users like Cathy, who travel across the states, should bear in mind that it is illegal to transport cannabis over state lines, and the drug remains illegal on federal property. The penalty for possessing cannabis in North Carolina depends on the type, how much she has, and how she plans to use it. In Cathy's case, she can possess up to 1.5 ounces of cannabis for personal use and a maximum of 0.15 ounces of hash or concentrates. All hemp-derived products, including CBD, are legal in the state if they contain less than 0.3 percent delta-9 THC. The federally legal alternative for cannabis, known as delta-8 THC, is the only legal cannabis product in North Carolina, again it must contain less than 0.3 percent delta-9 THC. It can be found easily in the state's local hemp stores and online.

However, if Cathy needs something more substantial, she must travel out of state or to the state's first dispensary on Cherokee Indian tribal land in the Great Smoky Mountain. The dispensary opened on April 20, 2024. Cathy can now travel to this site and consume medical cannabis there. Before she travels there, she will still need to obtain a certificate, attested by her doctor, for her medical conditions. She can apply for this online. Her insurance company will not cover her purchases as it is still illegal in North Carolina and federally. As pointed out in Chapter 9, the US Supreme Court voted that despite the irony, Congress had the legal authority to make the use of home-grown marijuana a criminal offense, even in states where it is legal for therapeutic purposes. As a result, Cathy and others like her who use or access medical cannabis in states that permit it are still vulnerable to criminal consequences.

However, she may not have to travel to the state's first dispensary in Cherokee or neighboring cannabis "friendly" states for too long. On May 1, 2024, the Federal Drug Enforcement Agency (DEA) announced a landmark move to remove cannabis from the Schedule I drug list and relist it as a Schedule III drug. The long-term implication of this move for people like Cathy is it will lead to the commercialization of cannabis drugs widely prescribed by conventional doctors and endorsed by insurance companies as prescription drugs.

In the medium to long run, Cathy need not move out of North Carolina because she can access specific advocacy organizations to support her right to use cannabis in her home state. Two such groups are the American Alliance for Medical Cannabis (AAMC) and the American Medical Marijuana Association (AMMA). Both groups promote and protect legal access to medical cannabis. The National Organization for the Reform of Marijuana Laws (NORML) is another national group that advocates for the reform of cannabis laws in the country. NORML Foundations is an affiliated group that emphasizes educating and providing legal aid to those adversely affected by existing cannabis laws. Any of these organizations will be able to help Cathy to continue using medical cannabis in her home state.

Directory of Resources

Books

Bollinger, T. (2016). *The truth about cancer: What you need to know about cancer's history, treatment, and prevention.* Hay House.

An excellent account of research showing the efficacy of unconventional cancer treatments that are helping patients around the world.

Bookman, M. Z., & Bookman, K. R. (2007). *Medical tourism in developing countries.* Palgrave MacMillan.

An analysis of the medical tourism market and exploration of its potential and implications.

Cohen, I. G. (2015). *Patients with passports: Medical tourism, law and ethics*, 1st edition. Oxford University Press.

A compelling narrative on the prevalent legal and ethical issues facing medical tourism today.

DeMicco, F. J. (Ed.). (2017). *Medical tourism and wellness: Hospitality bridging healthcare (H2H).* Apple Academic Press.

A systems approach through case studies in examining the industry from a medical and hospitality management perspective.

Gahlinger, P. (2008). *The medical tourism travel guide: Your complete reference to top-quality, low-cost dental, cosmetic, medical care & surgery overseas.* Sunrise River Press.

A unique account and guide on hundreds of healthcare facilities in about fifty countries, how to prepare for the trip and pay for it—what to do and what to avoid.

Grace, M. A. (2007). *State of the heart: A medical tourist's true story of lifesaving surgery in India.* New Harbinger.

A compelling personal account of a companion who travels with her partner to India to obtain a lifesaving surgery.

Hall, M. (Ed.). (2013). *Medical tourism: The ethics, regulation, and marketing of health mobility.* Routledge.

An overview of the political, philosophical, and ethical issues arising from the transnational practices of medical tourism.

Hammaker, D. K., Knadig, T. M., Gomberg, J. D. (2024). *Health care ethics and the law*, 2nd edition. Jones & Bartlett Learning.

A practical resource that presents ethical dilemmas based on actual court cases, and explains current and future trends in healthcare ethics and the law.

Hodges, J. R., Turner, L., & Kimball, A. M. (Eds.). (2016). *Risks and challenges in medical tourism: Understanding the global market for health services*. Praeger.

A comprehensive assessment of the benefits and risks when health care becomes a global commodity.

Lunt, N., Hanefeld, J., & Horsfall, D. (Eds.). (2015). *Elgar handbook on medical tourism and patient mobility*. Edward Elgar.

A handbook that explores the emergence of medical travel and patient mobility and the implications for patients and health systems.

Saupe, H. (2021). *Holistic cancer medicine: Integrative strategies for a new approach to health and healing*. Chelsea Green.

An excellent guide on less invasive natural cancer treatments for those seeking to prevent the disease and reduce their risks.

Schult, J. (2006). *Beauty from afar: A medical tourist's guide to affordable and quality cosmetic care outside the U.S.* Stewart, Tabori & Chang.

A personal account and guide that presents the pros and cons of traveling abroad for cosmetic or other elective surgeries.

Woodman, J. (2008). *Patients beyond borders: Everybody's guide to affordable, world-class medical travel*, 2nd edition. Healthy Travel Media.

The definitive manual for those planning a medical trip outside the US.

Magazines and News Journals

International Medical Travel Journal, https://www.imtj.com/.

News journals that provide insight into the medical tourism industry published by LaingBuisson, based in UK. It maintains a database of global healthcare providers and facilitators.

Medical Tourism Magazines, https://www.magazine.medicaltourism.com/.

Magazines published by Medical Tourism Association, based in West Palm Beach, Florida.

Accreditation Bodies

Accreditation Canada International (ACI), https://accreditation.ca/.

An organization that helps to improve the quality of health and social services in Canada and worldwide.

Australian Council on Healthcare Standards (ACHS), https://www.achs.org.au/.

An independent, not-for-profit organization dedicated to improving healthcare quality throughout Australia.

Global Healthcare Accreditation, https://www.globalhealthcareaccreditation.com/.

An accreditation body for stakeholders in workplace safety, health, and well-being.

International Society for Quality in Healthcare (IsQua), https://isqua.org/.

A nonprofit organization of people and institutions who are interested in the quality of health care. It accredits the accreditors through its International Accreditation Program.

Joint Commission International, https://www.jointcommissioninternational.org/.

An arm of the body that accredits most US hospitals to improve safety and quality of care.

Medical Travel Quality Alliance (MTQUA), http://www.mtqua.org/.

An independent organization that certifies healthcare providers, facilitators, and services in quality of care, and services to medical tourists.

QHA Trent Accreditation, https://www.qha-trent.co.uk/.

Based in the UK, it provides an expert-led, evidence-based, reasonably priced and transparent accreditation scheme for healthcare providers.

Temos International GmbH, https://www.temos-worldwide.com/.

A German-based accreditation body that offers accreditation programs for international healthcare providers, facilitators, rehabilitation centers, and pharmacies.

Treatment Abroad's Code of Practice, https://www.imtj.com/organisation/treatment-abroads-code-of-practice/.

It encourages the development of best practices amongst medical tourism agencies and healthcare providers.

Organizations

American Medical Association (AMA), https://www.ama-assn.org/press-center/press-releases/ama-adopts-ethical-guidance-medical-tourism.

It provides ethical guidelines for medical tourism.

American Society of Plastic Surgery (ASPS), https://www.plasticsurgery.org/news/plastic-surgery-statistics.

It provides useful annual statistics on plastic surgery.

Centers for Disease Control and Prevention, https://www.cdc.gov/.

It provides resources on various health topics including infertility, cannabis. It also provides the latest information on communicative diseases, especially that affecting those traveling outside the United States.

National Center for Complementary and Alternative Medicine (NCCIH), https://www.nccih.nih.gov/.

NCCIH conducts and supports research and provides information on complementary health practices and products.

Society for Assisted Reproductive Technology (SART), https://www.sart.org/.

SART is an organization of professionals dedicated to the practice of IVF. It publishes a national summary report on IVF practices in the United States.

World Bank Group, https://www.worldbank.org/en/home.

A group that works to find sustainable solutions to reduce poverty in developing countries. It also tracks and publishes socioeconomic data worldwide including healthcare expenditures.

World Health Organization (WHO), https://www.who.int/.

A branch of the United Nations that coordinates the world's response to health emergencies, prevents disease and expands access to healthcare. It publishes facts and statistics on various international health issues including infertility and density of doctors.

Useful Websites

American Alliance for Medical Cannabis (AAMC), http://letfreedomgrow.org/.

An organization that helps patients, caregivers and volunteers to make informed decisions about medical cannabis. It advocates and promotes legal access to medical cannabis.

American Medical Marijuana Association (AMMA), https://americanmarijuana.org/.

A valuable resource for up-to-date news on state cannabis laws and educational resources for those seeking medical cannabis.

Center for Medical Tourism Research, University of the Incarnate World, http://www.uiw.edu/medical-tourism/index.html.

A research center that conducts research on medical tourism, medical devices, and more.

Homewatch CareGiver, https://www.homewatchcaregivers.com/.

A franchisee of Homewatch International, Inc. It provides home care services for people of all ages and has more than 200 franchise locations in seven countries.

KFF, https://www.kff.org/other/state-indicator/abortion-policy-tracker/.

An independent source for health policy research, polling, and news. It tracks the abortion policies of various states in the United States.

Medical Tourism Research Center, University of North Carolina at Pembroke, https://www.uncp.edu/mtrc.

A research center that conducts research on medical tourism. It provides useful educational resources such as a current list of international hospitals and facilitators, and providers in complementary and alternative medicine.

National Conference of State Legislatures (NCSL), https://www.ncsl.org/health/state-medical-cannabis-laws#anchor8841.

A valuable resource for tracking the evolving state medical cannabis laws.

National Organization for the Reform of Marijuana Laws (NORML), https://norml.org/.

A social group that is based in Washington, DC. It advocates for the reform of cannabis laws in the United States for medical and nonmedical purposes.

Organdonor.gov, https://www.organdonor.gov/learn/organ-donation-statistics.

An interesting website that provides up-to-date statistics on organ donation, sponsored by Health Resources and Services Administration (HRSA).

The Moss Report, https://www.themossreport.com/.

Independent research and is a valuable resource for those who are seeking alternative cancer treatment. It requires a subscription.

Treatment Abroad, http://www.treatmentabroad.com/.

A site that provides comprehensive information and conducts surveys on medical travel, based in the UK.

Glossary

Asymmetric information Refers to when one party in a transaction is in possession of more information than the other.

Cachexia A wasting disorder that causes extreme weight loss, muscle wasting, and loss of body fat.

Cryopreservation of embryos Freezing of embryos for later use in the IVF procedure.

Economies of scope Refers to when producing a wider variety of goods or services by the same company is more cost-effective than producing each good or service independently.

Foreign healthcare provider (FHP) Refers to an offshore facility that provides healthcare services or a foreign physician.

Free riding Too much information may be provided when people benefit from resources, goods, or services they do not pay for.

Fully insured (or fully funded) plan A health plan in which employers pay a fixed premium to a third-party commercial insurance carrier to cover medical claims for their employees. The carrier assumes the financial risk related to coverage, including claims processing and other administrative tasks. (compare with self-insured plan).

Halal Usually refer to food that are prepared using procedures, equipment, or utensils that have been cleaned according to the Islamic law.

Health Insurance Portability and Accountability Act (HIPAA) The Act was passed in 1996 to protect the privacy and security of health information. It applies to health information that is individually identifiable and is maintained or exchanged electronically or in hard copy.

Health maintenance organization (HMO) A type of health plan that has its own network of hospitals and doctors who provide services for a specific payment. Thus, allowing HMO to maintain costs for its members (compare with PPO).

The Health on the Net Foundation (HON) A nonprofit, nongovernmental organization that promotes reliable online health information. It is accredited to the United Nations Economic and Social Council and has official relations with the World Health Organization.

In vitro fertilization (IVF) A type of fertility treatment where an egg is fertilized by sperm in a test tube or elsewhere outside the body.

Joint Commission International (JCI) An international accrediting body that verifies quality and safety standards in compliance with international healthcare standards.

Medical tourism complications insurance Insurance that caters to specific needs of medical tourists, from flight delay, change of hotel stay, surgery delay, wrong surgery, comorbidity factors, poor results, or other unexpected occurrences.

Medical tourism facilitator (MTF) A middleman company that sources foreign healthcare providers and facilitates the medical tourism journey for potential patients.

Monopolistic competition A market structure in which many firms sell similar but differentiated products or services in terms of quality, branding, style, and reputation. The firms operate and price independently. Examples are grocery stores and hotels.

Non-maleficence A basic principle of medical ethics that requires physicians to do no harm or allow harm to be inflicted on a patient through neglect.

Positive externality An activity that should be encouraged more in a society as it benefits the society without everyone paying for its benefits. For example, beautiful landscaping in the neighborhood.

Preferred provider organization (PPO) A type of health plan that offers a network of providers at a certain rate. Unlike HMO, it gives its members the freedom to choose any healthcare provider from within or outside its network (compare with HMO).

Preimplantation genetic diagnosis (PGD) The procedure is used with IVF to identify gene disorders. It can also be used to provide information regarding the sex of embryos in gender selection.

Search cost The time, energy, and money that buyers and sellers in a market expend to find one another to engage in transactions.

Self-insured (or self-funded) plan A health plan in which employers act as their own insurers and set aside funds to cover medical claims and fees. They may choose to hire a third-party administrator (TPA) to handle claims processing and other administrative tasks (compare with fully insured plan).

Spatial knowledge Refers to where things are, the name of places, distances, and direction between the places, and the relational organizations between places. One may use this knowledge to get from home to work, to plan their travels between different places, and to give navigational directions to others.

Trickle-down economics The demand for medical tourism will create jobs, new technology, and infrastructure, thereby benefiting economic, social, healthcare, and other related industries in the destination economies.

TuiNa massage The use of a combination of hand and arm techniques to massage and realign the recipient's muscles, bones, ligaments, and tendons. These techniques include kneading, pressing, rolling, shaking, and stretching.

References

Acibadem Technology (2023). About us. Retrieved from https://acibademtechnology.com/about-us/, last visited November 8, 2023.

Adabi, K., Stern, C. S., Weichman, K. E., Garfein, E. S., Pothula, A., Draper, L., & Tepper, O. M. (2017). Population health implications of medical tourism. *Plastic & Reconstructive Surgery 140*(1): 66–74. doi: 10.1097/PRS.0000000000003459.

Al Salmani, K., Moss, E., Jones, D., Patel, R., Burney, I., & Evans, M. D. (2015). Frankincense as a potentially novel therapeutic agent in ovarian cancer. The 27th Lorne Cancer Conference, February 2015, Mantra Lorne, Lorne, Victoria, Australia. doi:10.13140/2.1.1016.2241.

Allied Market Research (2020). Market overview, November. Retrieved from https://www.alliedmarketresearch.com/medical-tourism-market, last visited May 12, 2023.

American Society of Plastic Surgery (2023). Plastic surgery statistics. Retrieved from https://www.plasticsurgery.org/news/plastic-surgery-statistics, last visited June 29, 2024.

American Medical Association (AMA) (2007). Medical travel outside the U.S. OMSS governing council report B, June. Retrieved from https://www.medretreat.com/templates/UserFiles/Files/AMA%20Report%20June%202007.pdf, last visited July 4, 2024.

ANA Ethics Advisory Board (2022). ANA position statement: Therapeutic use of marijuana and related cannabinoids. *OJIN: The Online Journal of Issues in Nursing 27*(1).

Annas, G. J. (1997). Reefer madness—the federal response to California's medical-marijuana law. *New England Journal of Medicine 337*(6): 435–9. doi:10.1056/NEJM199708073370621.

Ataoglu, L. (2012). In-person interview with International Business Development and Projects Supervisor, International Patient Services Department, Acibadem Healthcare Group, Istanbul, Turkey, July 2.

Bagetta, G., Morrone, L. A., Rombolà, L., Amantea, D., Russo, R., Berliocchi, L., & Corasaniti, M. T. (2010). Neuropharmacology of the essential oil of bergamot. *Fitoterapia 81*(6): 453–61. https://doi.org/10.1016/J.FITOTE.2010.01.013.

Beck, M. (2014). How to bring the price of health care into the open. *The Wall Street Journal*, February 23, p. R.1. https://www.wsj.com/articles/SB10001424052702303650204579375242842086688.

Better Health Channel (2024). Medical tourism and insurance. Retrieved from https://www.betterhealth.vic.gov.au/health/healthyliving/medical-tourism, last visited June 14, 2024.

Bifulco, M., & Pisanti, S. (2015). Medicinal use of cannabis in Europe: The fact that more countries legalize the medicinal use of cannabis should not become an argument for unfettered and uncontrolled use. *EMBO Report 16*(2):130–2. doi: 10.15252/embr.201439742.

Black, L. I., Barnes, P. M., Clarke, T. C., Stussman, B. J., & Nahin, R. L. (2018). Use of yoga, meditation, and chiropractors among U.S. children aged 4–17 years. NCHS Data Brief, no 324. Hyattsville, MD: National Center for Health Statistics. Retrieved from https://www.nccih.nih.gov/research/statistics/nhis/2017, last visited July 23, 2023.

Blake, A. (2018). Marijuana legalization favored by most voters, despite new DOJ stance: Poll. *Washington Times*, January 11. Retrieved from https://www.washingtontimes.com/news/2018/jan/11/marijuana-legalization-favored-by-most-voters-desp/, last visited June 12, 2024.

Bobinski, M. A., Hall, M., & Orentlicher, D. (2007). *Health care law and ethics*, 7th edition. Aspen Publishers.

Bochaton, A. (2015). Cross-border mobility and social networks: Laotians seeking medical treatment along the Thai border. *Social Science & Medicine 124*: 364–73. doi: 10.1016/j.socscimed.2014.10.022.

Boehm, K., Büssing, A., & Ostermann, T. (2012). Aromatherapy as an adjuvant treatment in cancer care—a descriptive systematic review. *African Journal of Traditional Complement Alternative Medicine 9*(4): 503–18. doi: 10.4314/ajtcam.v9i4.7. PMID: 23983386; PMCID: PMC3746639.

Bollinger, T. (2016). *The truth about cancer: What you need to know about cancer's history, treatment, and prevention*. Hay House.

Boucher, D. (2021). The impact of Covid19 on medical tourism. Zoom interview with Group Chief of Service Excellence, Aster DM Healthcare, Dubai, UAE, June 8.

Brouwer, W., Van Exel, J., Hermans, B., & Stoop, A. (2003). Should I stay or should I go? Waiting lists and cross-border care in the Netherlands. *Health Policy 63*(3): 289–98. doi:10.1016/S0168-8510(02)00120-3.

Budiani-Saberi, D. A., & Delmonico, F. L. (2008). Organ trafficking and transplant tourism: A commentary on the global realities. *American Journal of Transplant 8*(5): 925–9. doi: 10.1111/j.1600-6143.2008.02200.x.

Burge, P., Devlin, N., Appleby, J., Rohr, C., & Grant, J. (2005). London patient choice project evaluation: A model of patients' choices of hospital from stated and revealed preference choice data, London: Rand Europe/King's Fund/City University. Retrieved from https://www.rand.org/content/dam/rand/pubs/technical_reports/2005/RAND_TR230.pdf, last visited May 23, 2023.

Burkett, L. (2007). Medical tourism. Concerns, benefits, and the American legal perspective. *Journal of Legal Medicine 28*(2): 223–45. doi: 10.1080/01947640701357763.

Carrera, P. M., & Bridges, J. F. P. (2006). Globalization and healthcare: Understanding health and medical tourism. *Expert Review of Pharmacoeconomics Outcomes Research* 6(4): 447–54.

Capelouto, S. M., Archer, S. R., Morris, J. R.,Kawwass, J. F., & Hipp, H. S. (2018). Sex selection for non-medical indications: A survey of current pre-implantation genetic screening practices among U.S. ART clinics. *Journal of Assisted Reproductive Genetics 35*(3): 409–16. doi: 10.1007/s10815-017-1076-2.

Centers for Disease Control and Prevention (2004). Brief report: Nontuberculous mycobacterial infections after cosmetic surgery—Santo Domingo, Dominican Republic, 2003–2004. *Morbidity and Mortality Weekly Report 53*: 509.

Centers for Disease Control and Prevention (2023). Fungal meningitis outbreak associated with procedures performed under epidural anesthesia in Matamoros, Mexico. Retrieved from https://archive.cdc.gov/www_cdc_gov/hai/outbreaks/meningitis-epidural-anesthesia.html, last visited June 14, 2024.

Centers for Disease Control and Prevention (2024a). Infertility: Frequently asked questions, May 15. Retrieved from https://www.cdc.gov/reproductive-health/infertility-faq/, last visited June 14, 2024.

Centers for Disease Control and Prevention (2024b). Cannabis facts and stat, February 22. Retrieved from https://www.cdc.gov/cannabis/data-research/facts-stats/?CDC_AAref_Val=https://www.cdc.gov/marijuana/data-statistics.htm, last visited June 14, 2024.

Centers for Medicare and Medicaid services (2022). Historical, December 15. Retrieved from https://www.cms.gov/research-statistics-data-and-systems/statistics-trends-and-reports/nationalhealthexpenddata/nationalhealthaccountshistorical, last visited May 12, 2023.

Cha, A. E. (2018). From sex selection to surrogates, American IVF clinics provide services outlawed elsewhere. *Washington Post*, December 30. Retrieved from https://www.washingtonpost.com/national/health-science/from-sex-selection-to-surrogates-american-ivf-clinics-provide-services-outlawed-elsewhere/2018/12/29/0b596668-03c0-11e9-9122-82e98f91ee6f_story.html, last visited June 12, 2024.

Chen, Y. Y. B., & Flood, C. M. (2013). Medical tourism's impact on health care equity and access in low- and middle-income countries: Making the case for regulation. *Journal of Law, Medicine & Ethics 41*(1): 286–300. https://doi.org/10.1111/jlme.12019.

Cheung, I. K., & Wilson, A. (2007). Arthroplasty tourism. *Medical Journal of Australia 187*(11–12): 666–7. doi.org/10.5694/j.1326-5377.2007.tb01467.x.

Chinai, R., & Goswami, R. (2007). Medical visas mark growth of Indian medical tourism. *Bulletin of the World Health Organization 85*(3): 164–5.

Chun, M. (2024). Virginia bills advance to protect state employees who access medical cannabis. *Capital News Service*, February 16. Retrieved from https://virginiamercury.com/2024/02/16/virginia-bills-advance-to-protect-state-employees-who-access-medical-cannabis/, last visited April 7, 2024.

Clark, P. A. (2000). The ethics of medical marijuana: Government restrictions vs. medical necessity. *Journal of Public Health Policy 21*(1): 40–60. PMID: 10754797.

Clarke, T. C., Barnes, P. M., Black, L. I., Stussman, B. J., & Nahin, R. L. (2018). Use of yoga, meditation, and chiropractors among U.S. adults aged 18 and over. NCHS Data Brief, no 325. Hyattsville, MD: National Center for Health Statistics. Retrieved from https://www.nccih.nih.gov/research/statistics/nhis/2017/yoga-meditation-use-adults, last visited July 23, 2023.

Cohen, I. G. (2010). Medical tourism: The view from ten thousand feet. *Hastings Center Report 40*(2): 11–12. doi: 10.1353/hcr.0.0238.

Corasaniti, M. T., Bagetta, G., Morrone, L. A., Tonin, P., Hamamura, K., Hayashi, T., Guida, F., Maione, S., & Scuteri, D. (2023). Efficacy of essential oils in relieving cancer pain: A systematic review and meta-analysis. *International Journal of Molecular Sciences 24*(8): 7085. doi: 10.3390/ijms24087085.

Cortez, N. (2012). Into the void: The legal ambiguities of an unregulated medical tourism market. In *Risks and challenges in medical tourism: Understanding the global market for health services* (ed. Jill Hodges, Leigh Turner, and Ann Marie Kimball). Praeger, pp. 187–206.

Crooks, V. A., Cohen, I. G., Adams, K., Whitmore, R., & Morgan, J. (2015). Inbound medical tourism to Barbados: A qualitative examination of local lawyers' prospective legal and regulatory concerns. *BMC Health Services Research 15*(1): 1–8. https://doi.org/10.1186/s12913-015-0948-3.

Crooks, V. A., & Snyder, J. (2010). Regulating medical tourism. *The Lancet 376*(9751): 1465–6. doi: https://doi.org/10.1016/S0140-6736(10)61993-9.

Crush, J., & Chikanda, A. (2015). South-South medical tourism and the quest for health in Southern Africa. *Social Science & Medicine 124*: 313–20. doi: 10.1016/j.socscimed.2014.06.025.

Deloitte (2008). Medical tourism: Consumers in search of value. Deloitte Center for Health Solutions.

Deloitte (2009). Medical tourism: Update and implications. Deloitte Center for Health Solutions.

Deloitte (2011). 2011 Survey of health care consumers global report: Key findings, strategic implications. Deloitte Center for Health Solutions.

DeNavas-Walt, C., Proctor, B. D., & Smith, J. C. (2010). Income, poverty, and health insurance coverage in the United States: 2009. *U.S. Census Bureau*, 60–238.

Eggertson L. (2006). Wait-list weary Canadians seek treatment abroad. *Canadian Medical Association Journal 174*(9): 1247. doi: 10.1503/cmaj.060219.

Elinson, Z., & Vielkind, J. (2023). How New York and California botched marijuana legalization. *Wall Street Journal*, April 28. Retrieved from https://www.wsj.com/articles/marijuana-legalization-dispensary-california-new-york-db1bb11c, last visited April 23, 2024.

Ethics Committee of the Society for Reproductive Medicine (2022). Use of reproductive technology for sex selection for nonmedical reasons: An ethics committee opinion. *Fertility and Sterility 117*(4): 720–6. doi: 10.1016/j.fertnstert.2021.12.024.

Forgione, D. A., & Smith, P. C. (2006). Medical tourism and its impact on the US health care system. *Journal of Health Care Finance 34*(1): 27–35.

Frank, R., Bernanke, B., Gan, L. & Chen, K. (2009). *Principles of economics*, Asian edition, McGrawHill.

Frass, M., Lechleitner, P., Gründling, C., Pirker, C., Grasmuk-Siegl, E., Domayer, J., Hochmair, M., Gaertner, K., Duscheck, C., Muchitsch, I., Marosi, C., Schumacher, M., Zöchbauer-Müller, S., Manchanda, R. K., Schrott, A., & Burghuber, O. (2020). Homeopathic treatment as an add-on therapy may improve quality of life and prolong survival in patients with non-small cell lung cancer: A prospective, randomized, placebo-controlled, double-blind, three-arm, multicenter study. *Oncologist 25*(12): e1930–55. doi: 10.1002/onco.13548.

Frederick, J., & Gan, L. (2015). East-west differences among medical tourism facilitators' websites. *Journal of Destination Marketing & Management 4*: 98–109. https://doi.org/10.1016/j.jdmm.2015.03.002.

Gahlinger, P. (2008). *The medical tourism travel guide: Your complete reference to top-quality, low-cost dental, cosmetic, medical care & surgery overseas*. Sunrise River Press.

Gallup (2023a). Where do Americans stand on abortions? Short Answers, July 7. Retrieved from https://news.gallup.com/poll/321143/americans-stand-abortion.aspx, last visited February 5, 2024.

Gallup (2023b). Moral issues, May 1–24. Retrieved from https://news.gallup.com/poll/1681/moral-issues.aspx, last visited February 24, 2024.

Gan, L., & Frederick, J. (2011). Medical tourism facilitators: Patterns of service differentiation. *Journal of Vacation Marketing 17*(3): 165–83. https://doi.org/10.1177/1356766711409181.

Gan, L., & Frederick, J. (2013a). Medical tourists: Who goes and what motivates them? *Healthcare Marketing Quarterly 30*(2): 177–94. https://doi.org/10.1080/07359683.2013.787894.

Gan, L., & Frederick, J. (2013b). The participation of medical tourism by US insurance companies. Unpublished study.

Gan, L. (2013c). The four modes of medical tourism: Economics, social and institutional impediments. In *Medical tourism: The ethics, regulation, and marketing of health mobility* (ed. Michael Hall). Routledge, pp. 47–60.

Gan, L., & Frederick, J. (2015). Regional differences: Scope and trust among medical tourism facilitators. In *Elgar Handbook on Medical Tourism and Patient Mobility* (ed. Neil Lunt, Johanna Hanefeld, and Daniel Horsfall). Edward Elgar, pp. 141–53.

Gan, L., & Frederick, J. (2018). The choice of facilitators in medical tourism. *Healthcare Marketing Quarterly 35*(3): 503–17. https://doi.org/10.1080/07359683.2018.1434891.

Gan, L. (2020). Medical tourism: Consumer motivation to travel for treatment post-covid-19. *Health and medical tourism 2020 virtual conference*, Dubai, United Arab Emirates, July 23–4.

Galentine, E. (2013). Medical travel regroups. *Employee Benefit Adviser 11*(6): 42.

Gautam, P. L., Kathuria, S., & Chhabra, S. (2011). Hot climate and perioperative outcome in elderly patients. *Indian Journal of Critical Care Medicine 15*(2): 88–95. doi: 10.4103/0972-5229.83013.

Giacomino, B. D., Cram, P., Vaughan-Sarrazin, M., Zhou, Y., & Girotra, S. (2016). Association of hospital prices for coronary artery bypass grafting with hospital quality and reimbursement. *American Journal of Cardiology 117*(7): 1101–6. doi: 10.1016/j.amjcard.2016.01.004.

Gianfaldoni, S., Tchernev, G., Wollina, U., Roccia, M. G., Fioranelli, M., Gianfaldoni, R., Lotti, T. (2017). History of the baths and thermal medicine. *Open Access Macedonians Journal of Medical Sciences 5*(4): 566–8. doi: 10.3889/oamjms.2017.126. PMCID: PMC5535692.

GlobeNewswire (2019). Herbal medicine market value to surpass USD 129 billion revenue mark by 2023 at 5.88% CAGR, predicts market research future. Market Research Future, April 3. Retrieved from https://www.globenewswire.com/en/news-release/2019/04/03/1796359/0/en/Herbal-Medicine-Market-Value-to-Surpass-USD-129-Billion-Revenue-Mark-by-2023-at-5-88-CAGR-Predicts-Market-Research-Future.html, last visited June 12, 2024.

Goddard, I., & Aragao, C. (2023). A growing share of Americans say they've had fertility treatments or know someone who has. Pew Research Center, September 14. Retrieved from https://www.pewresearch.org/short-reads/2023/09/14/a-growing-share-of-americans-say-theyve-had-fertility-treatments-or-know-someone-who-has/, last visited June 12, 2024.

Gooding, S. (1995). The relative importance of information sources in consumers' choice of hospitals. *Journal of Ambulatory Care Marketing 6*(1): 99–108. doi: 10.1300/j273v06n01_07.

Goodrich, J. N., & Goodrich, G. E. (1987). Health-care tourism—an exploratory study. *Tourism Management 8*: 217–22.

Green, T. V. (2022). Americans overwhelmingly say marijuana should be legal for medical or recreational use. Pew Research Center, November 22. Retrieved from https://www.pewresearch.org/short-reads/2022/11/22/americans-overwhelmingly-say-marijuana-should-be-legal-for-medical-or-recreational-use/, last visited June 12, 2024.

Grinspoon, P. (2022). Beyond CBD: Here come the other cannabinoids, but where's the evidence? Harvard Health Blog, September 26. Retrieved from https://www.health.harvard.edu/blog/beyond-cbd-here-come-the-other-cannabinoids-but-wheres-the-evidence-2021032322190, last visited April 21, 2024.

Gulf Business (2023). Dubai welcomes 674,000 medical tourists in 2022. April 12. Retrieved from https://gulfbusiness.com/dubai-received-674000-medical-tourists-in-2022/, last visited June 12, 2024.

Gunja, M. Z., Gumas, E. D., & Williams II, R. D. (2023). U.S. heath care from a global perspective, 2022: Accelerating spending, worsening outcomes. *Commonwealth Fund*, January 31. Retrieved from https://www.commonwealthfund.org/publications/issue-briefs/2023/jan/us-health-care-global-perspective-2022, last visited July 14, 2024.

Guttmacher Institute (2024). Medication abortions accounted for 63% of all US abortions in 2023, an increase from 53% in 2020. *News Release*, March 19. Retrieved from https://www.guttmacher.org/news-release/2024/medication-abortions-accounted-63-all-us-abortions-2023-increase-53-2020, last visited April 8, 2024.

Hancianu, M., Cioanca, O., Mihasan, M., & Hritcu, L. (2013). Neuroprotective effects of inhaled lavender oil on scopolamine-induced dementia via anti-oxidative activities in rats. *Phytomedicine 20*(5): 446–52. doi: 10.1016/j.phymed.2012.12.005.

Harvard Stem Cell Institute (2023). Stem cell tourism: False hope for real money. Retrieved from https://hsci.harvard.edu/stem-cell-tourism, last visited May 23, 2023.

Hazarika, I. (2009). Medical tourism: Its potential impact on the health workforce and health systems in India. *Health Policy and Planning 25*(3): 248–51.

Health-tourism.com (2022). The history of medical tourism. Retrieved from https://www.health-tourism.com/medical-tourism/history/, last visited May 13, 2023.

Herissone-Kelly, P. (2006). The prohibition of sex selection for social reasons in the United Kingdom: Public opinion trumps reproductive liberty? *Cambridge Quarterly Healthcare Ethics 15*(3): 261–72. doi: 10.1017/s0963180106060336.

Hershberger, P. E., & Pierce, P. F. (2010). Conceptualizing couples' decision making in PGD: Emerging cognitive, emotional, and moral dimensions. *Patient Education Counseling 81*(1): 53–62. doi: 10.1016/j.pec.2009.11.017.

Hery, D., Schwarte, B., Patel, K., Elliott, J. O., & Vasko, S. (2023). Plastic surgery tourism: Complications, costs, and unnecessary spending? *Aesthetic Surgery Journal Open Forum*, December 21. doi: 10.1093/asjof/ojad113.

Holliday, R., Bell, D., Cheung, O., Jones, M., & Probyn, E. (2015). Brief encounters: Assembling cosmetic surgery tourism. *Social Science & Medicine 124*: 298–304. doi:10.1016/j.socscimed.2014.06.047.

Horrigan, B., Lewis S., Abrams D. I., & Pechura C. (2012). Integrative medicine in America—How integrative medicine is being practiced in clinical centers across the United States. *Global Advances in Health and Medicine 1*(3): 18–94. doi: 10.7453/gahmj.2012.1.3.006.

Horton, S., & Cole, S. (2011). Medical returns: Seeking health care in Mexico. *Social Science and Medicine 72*(11): 1846–52. doi: 10.1016/j.socscimed.2011.03.035.

Hudson, K., Scott, J., & Kalfoglou, A. (2002). Public awareness and attitudes about reproductive genetic technology. *Genetics and Public Policy Center*, December

9. Retrieved from https://jscholarship.library.jhu.edu/handle/1774.2/979, last visited June 13, 2024.

Hutchinson, B. (2005). Medical tourism growing worldwide. *UD Messenger 13*(4), University of Delaware. Retrieved from https://www1.udel.edu/PR/Messenger/04/04/medical.html, last visited May 18, 2024.

Inci, D. (2012). In-person interview with International Services Supervisor, Anadolu Medical Centre (affiliated with Johns Hopkins Medicine), Istanbul, Turkey, July 3.

International Society of Aesthetic Plastic Surgery (ISAPS) (2021). Global survey 2021: Full report and press releases. Retrieved from https://www.isaps.org/media/vdpdanke/isaps-global- survey_2021.pdf, last visited July 4, 2024.

International Trade Administration (2024). Turkey—Country commercial guide: Medical technologies and health IT, January 6. Retrieved from https://www.trade.gov/country-commercial-guides/turkey-medical-technologies-and-health-it, last visited July 17, 2024.

Iorio, M. L., Verma, K., Ashktorab, S., & Davison, S. P. (2014). Medical tourism in plastic surgery: Ethical guidelines and practice standards for perioperative care. *Aesthetic Plastic Surgery 38*(3): 602–7. doi: 10.1007/s00266-014-0322-6.

Javalgi, R., Rao, S., & Thomas, E. (1991). Choosing a hospital: Analysis of consumer tradeoffs. *Journal of Health Care Marketing 11*(1): 12–22. doi:10.110076.

Jayanetti, C. (2022). NHS hospital wait times above 18 weeks at a third of departments. *The Guardian*, August 27. Retrieved from https://www.theguardian.com/society/2022/aug/27/nhs-hospital-wait-times-above-18-weeks-at-a-third-of-departments, last visited June 13, 2024

Jeevan, R., & Armstrong, A. (2008). Cosmetic tourism and the burden on the NHS. *Journal of Plastic, Reconstructive and Aesthetic Surgery 61*(12): 1423–4.

Jin, K. (2021). The impact of Covid19 on medical tourism. Zoom interview with director of South Korea Council of Medical Tourism, Seoul, South Korea, June 3.

Johnson, G., Selsky, A., & Blood, M. (2023). Ganja glut? With excess weed, growers seek interstate sales. *Associated press*, April 19. Retrieved from https://apnews.com/article/cannabis-marijuana-420-legal-california-oregon-washington-ae7880387eee7dbfcfecaff563d0b211, last visited June 12, 2024.

Johnston, R., Crooks, V. A., Snyder, J., & Kingsbury, P. (2010). What is known about the effects of medical tourism in destination and departure countries? A scoping review. *International Journal of Equity in Health 9*(24): 1–13. doi.org/10.1186/1475-9276-9-24.

KFF (2023). Abortion policy tracker. State health facts, November 2. Retrieved from https://www.kff.org/other/state-indicator/abortion-policy-tracker/, last visited June 13, 2024.

Khartan, A. (2021). The impact of Covid19 on medical tourism. Zoom interview with Manager of Public Relations, Jordan Hospital, Amman, Jordan, July 1.

Kher, U. (2006). Outsourcing your heart. Time Magazine, May 21. Retrieved from https://content.time.com/time/subscriber/article/0,33009,1196429-3,00.html

Knef, S. (2022). CBD store owners says Kentuckians may struggle to obtain medical cannabis. *Spectrum News*, December 5. Retrieved from https://spectrumnews1.com/ky/louisville/news/2022/12/05/how-to-get-medical-cannabis, last visited June 27, 2024.

Knowledge at Wharton Podcast (2009). Bangkok's Bumrungrad Hospital: Expanding the footprint of offshore health care, September 2. Retrieved from https://knowledge.wharton.upenn.edu/podcast/knowledge-at-wharton-podcast/bangkoks-bumrungrad-hospital-expanding-the-footprint-of-offshore-health-care/, last visited November 29, 2023.

Kortsmit K., Nguyen A. T., Mandel M. G., Clark, E., Hollier, L. M., Rodenhizer, J., & Whiteman, M. K. (2022). Abortion surveillance—United States, 2020. CDC's Morbidity and mortality report weekly report (MMWR) surveillance summary, November 25, 71 (No. SS-10):1–27. DOI: http://dx.doi.org/10.15585/mmwr.ss7110a1.

Labonté, R., Crooks, V. A., Valdés, A. C., Runnels, V., & Snyder, J. (2018). Government roles in regulating medical tourism: Evidence from Guatemala. *International Journal of Equity Health 17*(150): 1–10. https://doi.org/10.1186/s12939-018-0866-1.

Lagiewski, R. M., & Myers, W. (2008). Medical tourism: Perspectives and applications for destination development. *RIT Scholar Works*. Retrieved from https://scholarworks.rit.edu/other/683/.

Lee, Jaeeun (2023). Medical tourists returning to South Korea: Data. *Korea Herald*, April 24. Retrieved from https://www.koreaherald.com/view.php?ud=20230424000602#, last visited June 3, 2023.

Lee, H., Wright, K. B., O'Connor, M., & Wombacher, K. (2014). Framing medical tourism: An analysis of persuasive appeals, risks and benefits, and new media features of medical tourism broker websites. *Health Communication 29*(7): 637–45. doi: 10.1080/10410236.2013.794412.

Lee, J. Y., Kearns, R., & Friesen, W. (2010). Seeking affective healthcare: Korean immigrants' use of homeland medical services. *Health & Place 16*: 108–15. doi:10.1016/j.healthplace.2009.09.003.

Leonhardt, M. (2019). Women are traveling far and wide for affordable IVF—here's why it's so expensive. *CNBC Make It*, August 13. Retrieved from https://www.cnbc.com/2019/08/13/women-are-traveling-far-and-wide-for-affordable-ivf.html, last visited June 14, 2024.

Lieman, H. J., & Breborowicz, A. K. (2014). Sex selection for family balancing. *Virtual Mentor 16*(10): 797–802. doi: 10.1001/virtualmentor.2014.16.10.ecas3-1410.

Loss, L. (2023). Five out of 100 tourists traveling to Turkey for health tourism. *Tourism Review News*, August 13. Retrieved from https://www.tourism-review.com/traveling-to-turkey-for-health-tourism-trend-news13540, last visited November 7, 2023.

Lytel, J. (2012). Medical tourism doesn't necessarily mean leaving the country to get treatment. *Washington Post*, October 29. Retrieved from https://www.washingtonpost.com/national/health-science/medical-tourism-doesnt-necessarily-mean-leav ing-the-country-to-get-treatment/2012/10/29/8d1bf5ce-d679-11e1-b2d5-2419d22 7d8b0_story.html, last visited June 12, 2024.

Maddow-Zimet, I., & Gibson, C. (2024). Despite bans, number of abortions in the United States increased in 2023. *Policy Analysis, Guttmacher Institute*, updated May 10. Retrieved from https://www.guttmacher.org/2024/03/despite-bans-number-abortions-united-states-increased-2023, last visited June 14, 2024.

Manneh, S. A. (2021). The impact of Covid19 on medical tourism. Zoom interview with Marketing & Business Development Manager, Specialty hospital, Jordan, June 14.

Marlowe, J., & Sullivan, P. (2007). Medical tourism: The ultimate outsourcing. *Human Resource Physician Executive 33*(6): 24–30.

Mattoo, A., & Rathindran, R. (2006). How health insurance inhibits trade in health care. *Health Affairs 25*(2): 358–68. https://doi.org/10.1377/hlthaff.25.2.358.

Matthews, F., & Freund, A. (2022). Virtual health could move destination medicine to the next level. *Deloitte Healthcare Blog*, August 11. Retrieved from https://www2.deloitte.com/us/en/blog/health-care-blog/2022/virtual-health-could-move-destination-medicine-to-the-next-level.html, last visited May 12, 2023.

McLean, T. R. (2007). Commentary: The industrialization of medical tourism and the Blue Ridge paper claim. *Journal of Controversial Medical Claims 14*(1): 18–19.

Medical Tourism Corporation (2024). Medical tourism insurance for bariatric surgery in Mexico. Retrieved from https://www.medicaltourismco.com/medical-tourism-insurance-for-bariatric-surgery-in-mexico, last visited June 4, 2024.

Medical Tourism Magazine (2010). Medical tourism—An engine to growth in the consumption of medical equipment. Retrieved from https://www.magazine.medicaltourism.com/article/medical-tourism-an-engine-to-growth-in-the-consumption-of-medical-equipment, last visited July 17, 2024.

Medical Tourism Magazine (2014). Health insurers turn to medical tourism strategies to bypass Obamacare, July. Retrieved from https://www.magazine.medicaltourism.com/article/health-insurers-look-medical-tourism-transparent-strategy-face-obamacare, last visited May 22, 2024.

Metri, K., Bhargav, H., Chowdhury, P., & Koka, P. S. (2013). Ayurveda for chemo-radiotherapy induced side effects in cancer patients. *Journal of Stem Cells 8*(2): 115–29. PMID: 24698988.

Meštrović, T. (2023). Employer-sponsored medical tourism, June 12. Retrieved from https://www.news-medical.net/health/Employer-Sponsored-Medical-Tourism.aspx, last visited May 16, 2024.

Milstein, A., & Smith, M. (2006). America's new refugees: Seeking affordable surgery offshore. *New England Journal of Medicine 355*(16): 1637–40.

Miller, A., Smith, R., Woods, N., & Warholak, T. (2020). Analysis of medical tourism at the Andrade port of entry. *Journal of the American Pharmacists Association 61*(2): e114–19. https://doi.org/10.1016/j.japh.2020.10.018.

Miller, P. (2022). New survey: Physician appointment wait times getting longer. *AMN Healthcare blog*, September 12. Retrieved from https://www.amnhealthcare.com/

blog/physician/perm/physician-appointment-wait-times-getting-longer/, last visited June 9, 2024.

Mirrer-Singer, P. (2007). Medical malpractice overseas: The legal uncertainty surrounding medical tourism. *Law and Contemporary Problems 70*(2): 211–32.

Mizuno, D., Kawahara, M., Konoha-Mizuno, K., & Yamazaki, K. (2022). Enhancing cytotoxicity of Tamoxifen Using *geranium* oil. *Evidence Based Complementary Alternative Medicine*.8091339. doi: 10.1155/2022/8091339.

Moir, M., & Barua, B. (2022). Waiting your turn: Wait times for health care in Canada, 2022 report. Fraser Institute, December 8. Retrieved from https://www.fraserinstitute.org/sites/default/files/waiting-your-turn-2022.pdf, last visited May 26, 2023.

The Moss Report (n.d.). Acupuncture for cancer. Retrieved from https://www.themossreport.com/acupuncture-for-cancer/, lasted visited July 17, 2023.

Mudur, G. (2004). Hospitals in India woo foreign patients. *British Medical Journal 326*: 520.

Naik, S. (2023). Over 1.4 million medical tourists visited India in 2022. *Economic Times*, April 18. Retrieved from https://travel.economictimes.indiatimes.com/news/ministry/over-1-4-mn-medical-tourists-visited-india-in-2022-shripad-naik/99576687, last visited June 3, 2023.

National Center for Complementary and Alternative Medicine (2018). The use of complementary and alternative medicine in the United States. Retrieved from https://files.nccih.nih.gov/s3fs-public/camuse.pdf, last visited June 12, 2024.

National Conference of State Legislatures (2023). State medical cannabis laws. Updated June 22. Retrieved from https://www.ncsl.org/health/state-medical-cannabis-laws#anchor8841, last visited April 24, 2024.

National Institute of Health (1997). National Institute on Drug Abuse, Report to the Director. Bethesda, MD: Workshop on the medical utility of marijuana.

Naujokat, C., & McKee, D. L. (2020). The "Big Five" phytochemicals targeting cancer stem cells: Curcumin, EGCG, sulforaphane, resveratrol, and genistein. *Current Medicinal Chemistry 28*(22): 4321–42. doi:10.2174/0929867327666200228110738.

Newman, D. J., & Cragg, G. M. (2020). Natural products as sources of new drugs over the nearly four decades from 01/1981 to 09/2019. *Journal of Natural Products 83*(3): 770–803. doi: 10.1021/acs.jnatprod.9b01285.

O'Neill, J. (2023). 1.2 million Americans visit Mexico for "medical tourism" each year. *New York Post*, March 8. Retrieved from https://nypost.com/2023/03/08/1-2m-americans-visit-mexico-for-medical-tourism-each-year/, last visited June 4, 2023.

Organdonor.gov (2024). Organ donation statistics. Retrieved from https://www.organdonor.gov/learn/organ-donation-statistics, last visited June 9, 2024.

Ormond, M., & Mainil, T. (2015). Government and governance strategies in medical tourism. In *Elgar Handbook on Medical Tourism and Patient Mobility* (ed. Neil Lunt, Johanna Hanefeld, and Daniel Horsfall). Edward Elgar, pp. 154–63.

Painter, K. (2024). Medical marijuana: Benefits and side effects. WebMd, January 9. Retrieved from https://www.webmd.com/a-to-z-guides/medical-marijuana-faq, last visited June 13, 2024.

Penney, K., Snyder, J., Crooks, V., & Johnston, R. (2011). Risk communication and informed consent in the medical tourism industry: A thematic content analysis of Canadian broker websites. *BMC Medical Ethics 12*(17): 1–9. doi:10.1186/1472-6939-12-17.

Pickert, K. (2008). Medical tourism. *Time*, November 25. Retrieved from https://time.com/archive/6932974/medical-tourism/, last visited June 14, 2024.

The Private Hospitals Association (n.d.). Healthcare system overview. Retrieved from https://phajordan.org/View_Article.aspx?type=2&ID=3809, last visited June 10, 2024.

Public Health Institute (2023). New research shows older adults are the fastest growing population to try marijuana, August 24. Retrieved from https://www.phi.org/press/new-research-shows-older-adults-are-the-fastest-growing-population-to-try-marijuana/, last visited June 14, 2024.

Raffles Medical Group (2023). Caring as one in Asia: Annual report 2023. Retrieved from https://www.rafflesmedicalgroup.com/wp-content/uploads/2024/04/RMG-Annual-Report-2023-caring-as-one-asia.pdf, last visited June 10, 2024.

Ramirez de Arellano, A. (2007). Patients without borders: The emergence of medical tourism. *International Journal of Health Services 37*(1): 193–8. doi: 10.2190/4857-468G-2325-47UU.

Rosenthal, J. (2009). Medical tourism takes off. *National Geographic Traveler 26*(4): 10–16.

Rothberg, M. B., Class, J., Bishop, T. F., Friderici, J., Kleppel, R., and Lindenauer, P. K. (2014). The cost of defensive medicine on 3 hospital medicine services. *Journal of American Medicine: Internal Medicine 174*(11): 1867– 8. doi: 10.1001/jamainternmed.2014.4649.

Sagy, I., Peleg-Sagy, T., Barski, L., Zeller, L., & Jotkowitz, A. (2018). Ethical issues in medical cannabis use. *European Journal of Internal Medicine 49*: 20–2. doi: 10.1016/j.ejim.2018.01.016.

Saupe, Henning (2021). *Holistic cancer medicine: Integrative strategies for a new approach to health and healing*. Chelsea Green.

Sharfstein, Joshua (2024). The Alabama supreme court's ruling on frozen embryos. *Public health on call podcast*, February 27. Retrieved from https://publichealth.jhu.edu/2024/the-alabama-supreme-courts-ruling-on-frozen-embryos, last visited June 13, 2024.

Shepherd, K. (2023). The difference between buying weed in D.C., Maryland and Virginia. *Washington Post*, May 3. Retrieved from https://www.washingtonpost.com/dc-md-va/2023/05/03/buying-weed-dc-maryland-virginia/, last visited April 23, 2024.

Sherwood, C. H. (2014). US states vie to lure medical tourists seeking healthcare alongside vacations. *The Guardian*, December 12. Retrieved from https://www.theguardian.com/business/2014/dec/12/us-states-vie-to-lure-medical-tourists-seeking-healthcare-alongside-vacations, last visited May 25, 2024.

Shimazono, Y. (2007). The state of the international organ trade: A provisional picture based on integration of available information. *Bulletin of World Health Organization 85*(12): 955–62. doi: 10.2471/blt.06.039370.

Sidhu, J. (2012). How to buy a daughter. *Slate*, September 14. Retrieved from https://slate.com/technology/2012/09/sex-selection-in-babies-through-pgd-americans-are-paying-to-have-daughters-rather-than-sons.html, last visited April 17, 2024.

Simmons-Duffin, S. (2024). Despite bans in some states, more than a million abortions were provided in 2023. NPR, March 19. Retrieved from https://www.capradio.org/articles/2024/03/19/despite-bans-in-some-states-more-than-a-million-abortions-were-provided-in-2023/, last visited June 12, 2024.

Simmons-Duffin, S., & Cheng, S. (2023). How many miles do you have to travel to get abortion care? One professor maps it. NPR, June 21. Retrieved from https://www.npr.org/sections/health-shots/2023/06/21/1183248911/abortion-access-distance-to-care-travel-miles, last visited June 12, 2024.

Smerd, J. (2008). Large companies hopping aboard medical tourism. *Workforce Management 87*(11): 8–10.

Society for Assisted Reproductive Technology (2017). National Summary Report. Retrieved from https://www.sartcorsonline.com/rptCSR_PublicMultYear.aspx?reportingYear=2017, last visited June 12, 2024.

Soo, L. Y. (2012). In-person interview with manager of hospital marketing, International Patient Centre, Raffles Hospital, Singapore, July 2.

Steinbock, B. (2024). Abortion. The Hastings Center, February 22. Retrieved from https://www.thehastingscenter.org/briefingbook/abortion/, last visited June 13, 2024.

Stolberg, S. G. (1999). Government study on marijuana sees medical benefits. *New York Times*, March 18. Retrieved from https://www.nytimes.com/1999/03/18/us/government-study-of-marijuana-sees-medical-benefits.html, last visited June 13, 2024.

Su, D., Richardson, C., Wen, M., & Pagan, J. A. (2011). Cross border utilization of healthcare: Evidence from a population-based study of South Texas. *Health Services Research 46*(3): 859–76. doi: 10.1111/j.1475-6773.2010.01220.x.

Tanner, L. (2022). Abortion law sparks profound changes in other medical care. *Associated Press*, July 16. Retrieved from https://apnews.com/article/abortion-science-health-medication-lupus-e4042947e4cc0c45e38837d394199033, last visited June 13, 2024.

Tena-Tamayo, C., & Sotelo, J. (2005). Malpractice in Mexico: Arbitration not litigation. *British Medical Journal 331*(7514): 448–51. doi: 10.1136/bmj.331.7514.448.

Thomas, G., & Krishnan, S. (2010). Effective public-private partnership in healthcare: Apollo as a cautionary tale. *Indian Journal of Medical Ethics 7*(1): 2–4. doi: 10.20529/IJME.2010.001.

Thorpe, K. E. (2005). The rise in health care spending and what to do about It. *Health Affairs 24*(6): 1436–45. doi: 10.1377/hlthaff.24.6.1436.

Thurstone, C., Lieberman, S. A., & Schmiege S. J. (2011). Medical marijuana diversion and associated problems in adolescent substance treatment. *Drug Alcohol Dependence 118*(2): 489–92. doi: 10.1016/j.drugalcdep.2011.03.031.

Totenberg, N., & McCammon, S. (2022). Supreme Court overturns Roe v. Wade, ending right to abortion upheld for decades. NPR, June 24. Retrieved from https://www.npr.org/2022/06/24/1102305878/supreme-court-abortion-roe-v-wade-decision-overturn, last visited June 14, 2024.

Tsai, B. (2023). U.S. uninsured rate hits record low in first quarter of 2023. Center for Disease Control and Prevention, August 3. Retrieved from https://blogs.cdc.gov/nchs/2023/08/03/7434/, last visited June 14, 2024.

Turner, L. (2007). First world health care at third world prices: Globalization, bioethics and medical tourism. *Bio Societies 2*: 303–25.

Üner, M. M., Çetin, B., Eroğlu, S., & Çavuşgil, S. T. (2021). Internationalization journey of healthcare providers: The case of Turkish Acıbadem healthcare group. *Thunderbird International Business Review 64*(1): 5–12. https://doi.org/10.1002/tie.22242.

United Nations World Tourism Organization (UNWTO) (2021). 2020: Worst year in tourism history with 1 billion fewer international arrivals, January 28. Retrieved from https://www.unwto.org/news/2020-worst-year-in-tourism-history-with-1-billion-fewer-international-arrivals, last visited June 10, 2024.

United Patients Group (2024). THC. Retrieved from https://unitedpatientsgroup.com/thc/, last visited July 24, 2024.

United States Department of Health and Human Services, National Institute of Mental Health. (USDHHS-NIMH) (2021). Mental illness. Retrieved from https://www.nimh.nih.gov/health/statistics/mental-illness.shtml, last visited July 23, 2024.

VCU CNS (2023). Virginia's medical cannabis program has "improved". *Capital News Service*, Virginia Commonwealth University, May 18. Retrieved from https://www.vpm.org/news/2023-05-18/medical-marijuana-virginia-shortcomings, last visited June 12, 2024.

Veerasoontorn, R., Beise-Zee, R., & Sivayathorn, A. (2011). Service quality as a key driver of medical tourism: The case of Bumrungrad International Hospital in Thailand. *International Journal of Leisure and Tourism Marketing 2*(2): 140 – 58. doi:10.1504/IJLTM.2011.038886.

Vijaya, R. M. (2010). Medical tourism: Revenue generation or international transfer of healthcare problems? *Journal of Economic Issues 44*(1): 53–70.

Wellable (2023). Study: 40% of employers now provide fertility benefits, increasing from 30% in 2020, March 13. Retrieved from https://www.wellable.co/blog/40-percent-of-employers-now-provide-fertility-benefits/, last visited June 14, 2024.

Whittaker, A. (2008). Pleasure and pain: Medical travel in Asia. *Global Public Health* *3*(3): 271–90. https://doi.org/10.1080/17441690701463936.

Whittaker, A. (2012). Cross-border assisted reproductive care. In *Risks and Challenges in Medical Tourism: Understanding the Global Market for Health Services* (ed. Jill Hodges, Leigh Turner, & Ann Marie Kimball). Praeger, pp. 167–83.

Whitlock, J. (2020). What you should know about medical tourism. *Verywell Health*, May 7. Retrieved from https://www.verywellhealth.com/understanding-medical-tourism-4069869, last visited June 9, 2024.

Whitlock, J. (2022). Why patients are turning to medical tourism: Statistics, benefits, and risks. *Verywell Health*, August 11. Retrieved from https://www.verywellhealth.com/understanding-medical-tourism-4069869, last visited June 9, 2024.

Wilson, C. (2009). Dis-embedding health care: Marketisation and the rising cost of medicine in Kerala, South India. *Journal of South Asian Development*, *4*(1), 83–101. https://doi.org/10.1177/097317410900400106

Wojcik, J. (2013). Medical tourism growing as employer health care option. *Business Insurance 47*(25): 8.

Woodman, J. (2008). *Patients beyond borders*, 2nd edition. Healthy Travel Media.

World Bank Group (2024a). Domestic private health expenditure (% of current health expenditure)—Thailand. Retrieved from https://data.worldbank.org/indicator/SH.XPD.GHED.CH.ZS?locations=TH, last visited July 4, 2024.

World Bank Group (2024b). Domestic private health expenditure (% of current health expenditure)—India. Retrieved from https://data.worldbank.org/indicator/SH.XPD.PVTD.CH.ZS?locations=IN, last visited July 4, 2024.

World Health Organization (2023). 1 in 6 people globally affected by infertility. *News Release*, April 4. Retrieved from https://www.who.int/news/item/04-04-2023-1-in-6-people-globally-affected-by-infertility, last visited June 10, 2024.

World Health Organization (2024). Density of physicians (per 10,000), May 20. Retrieved from https://data.who.int/indicators/i/CCCEBB2/217795A, last visited July 14, 2024.

Yang, J. (2024). Average percentage of Canadian patients who received medical treatment outside of Canada in 2023, by specialty. Statista. Retrieved from https://www.statista.com/statistics/654694/patients-receiving-treatment-outside-canada/, last visited May 16, 2024.

Yang, Y. (2011). Medical tourism in the eyes of insurance companies. PURC Symposium, University of North Carolina. Retrieved from https://libres.uncg.edu/ir/listing.aspx?id=7647, last visited June 27, 2024.

York, D. (2008). Medical tourism: The trend toward outsourcing medical procedures to foreign countries. *Journal of Continuing Education in the Health Professions* *28*(2): 99–102.

Younis, M. (2023). Most Americans favor availability of abortion pill. *Gallup News*, June 14. Retrieved from https://news.gallup.com/poll/507149/americans-favor-availability-abortion-pill.aspx, last visited June 12, 2024.

Index

About the Author

Lydia L. Gan, PhD, is a professor of Economics at the University of North Carolina at Pembroke. She teaches courses in health economics and principles of economics. She is also the cofounder and the research coordinator of the Medical Tourism Research Center at the University of North Carolina at Pembroke. Dr. Gan has written extensively on medical tourism, with around thirty journal articles and two book chapters. Her publications include contributions to *Elgar Handbook on Medical Tourism and Patient Mobility* (eds. Lunt, Hanefeld & Horsfall, 2015) and Routledge's *Medical Tourism: The Ethics, Regulation, and Marketing of Health Mobility* (ed. Hall, 2013). Additionally, she coauthored McGraw Hill's *Principles of Economics, Asian Edition* (Frank, Bernanke, Gan, & Chen, 2009). Dr. Gan's work on medical tourism has garnered international acclaim, and she has been consulted by organizations representing insurers, medical tourism agents, independent agencies, and news writers. Her research has taken her to various countries, such as Israel, Jordan, Malaysia, Singapore, South Africa, Thailand, and Turkey, where she visited hospitals and conducted interviews.